WALKI

# EASTE

Paul
Hannon

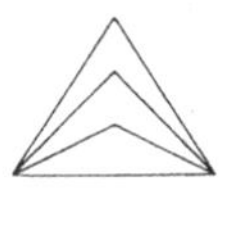

HILLSIDE

# HILLSIDE GUIDES - ACROSS THE NORTH

*Long Distance Walks*

•COAST TO COAST WALK •CLEVELAND WAY COMPANION
•WESTMORLAND WAY •FURNESS WAY •CUMBERLAND WAY
•DALES WAY •LADY ANNE'S WAY •NORTH BOWLAND TRAVERSE

*Circular Walks - Lancashire*

•BOWLAND •PENDLE & THE RIBBLE

*Circular Walks - Yorkshire Dales*

•HOWGILL FELLS •THREE PEAKS •MALHAMDALE
•WHARFEDALE •NIDDERDALE •WENSLEYDALE •SWALEDALE

*Circular Walks - North York Moors*

•WESTERN MOORS •SOUTHERN MOORS •NORTHERN MOORS

*Circular Walks - South Pennines*

•BRONTE COUNTRY •CALDERDALE •ILKLEY MOOR

*Circular Walks - Peak District*

•EASTERN PEAK • NORTHERN PEAK • CENTRAL PEAK
• SOUTHERN PEAK • WESTERN PEAK

*Circular Walks - North Pennines*

•TEESDALE •EDEN VALLEY

*Hillwalking - Lake District*

•OVER LAKELAND MOUNTAINS •OVER LAKELAND FELLS

*Yorkshire Pub Walks*

•HARROGATE/WHARFE VALLEY •HAWORTH/AIRE VALLEY

*Large format colour hardback*

**FREEDOM OF THE DALES**

*BIKING COUNTRY*

•YORKSHIRE DALES CYCLE WAY •WEST YORKSHIRE CYCLE WAY
•MOUNTAIN BIKING - WEST & SOUTH YORKSHIRE
•AIRE VALLEY BIKING GUIDE •CALDERDALE BIKING GUIDE
• GLASGOW Clyde Valley & Loch Lomond

• YORK WALKS *City Theme Walks*

•WALKING COUNTRY TRIVIA QUIZ *Over 1000 questions*

Send S.A.E. for a detailed catalogue and pricelist

WALKING COUNTRY

# EASTERN PEAK

Paul Hannon

HILLSIDE

**HILLSIDE**
**PUBLICATIONS**
11 Nessfield Grove
Keighley
West Yorkshire
BD22 6NU

First published 1997



ISBN 1 870141 50 4

Whilst the author has walked and researched all the routes for the purposes of this guide, no responsibility can be accepted for any unforeseen circumstances encountered while following them. The publisher would, however, greatly appreciate any information regarding material changes, and any problems encountered.

The author would like to acknowledge the assistance of Roland Smith, Head of Information Services at the Peak National Park, for his invaluable help in looking over the manuscript. Any errors, however, remain the author's.

*Cover illustrations:*
*Abbey Brook; Stanage Edge; Chatsworth*
*Back cover: On Higger Tor, Hathersage Moor*
*(Paul Hannon/Big Country Picture Library)*

*Page 1: Wellington's Monument, near Baslow Edge*
*Page 3: Lost Lad, Derwent Edge*

Printed in Great Britain by
Carnmor Print and Design
95-97 London Road
Preston
Lancashire
PR1 4BA

# CONTENTS

# INTRODUCTION

## THE PEAK NATIONAL PARK

The Peak District was designated Britain's first National Park in 1951, and embracing an area of 555 square miles it is the most popular in the country. While commonly allotted to Derbyshire, substantial parts fall within Staffordshire, Yorkshire and Cheshire. *Peak* is in fact a misnomer, for it is plainly evident that peaks are in very short supply here: it derives from *Pecsaetan* ('hill-dweller'), tribes that occupied the area long before the Normans came.

The Peak divides into two distinctive areas, the Dark Peak and the White Peak. These refer to the principal rocks, millstone grit (gritstone) in the Dark Peak and limestone in the White Peak. The Dark Peak horseshoe encloses the limestone country, with the high moors of Kinder Scout and Bleaklow to the north and long arms reaching down either side. That in the east traces the Derwent Valley south in a series of abrupt edges: that to the west is disjointed, resurrecting itself above Buxton to run south, largely less dramatically, west of the Manifold Valley. The northern massif is typified by vast tracts of peat bog and heather, a world away from the White Peak's softer terrain.

The compact White Peak offers green dales overlooked by gleaming cliffs. Unlike the limestone country of the Yorkshire Dales, it has few potholes and pavements: its speciality is valleys, exemplified by the likes of Lathkill Dale, the river Wye and the incomparable Dovedale. Much of the White Peak is an upland plateau where old lead mining communities huddle. The area is dissected by drystone walls, and though large-scale quarrying is all too evident, farming remains the traditional source of employment, increasingly supplemented by tourism. While one railway survives to run through the heart of the Park, several others have been converted to leisure trails: they provide excellent cross-country routes linking numerous towns and villages.

Bakewell is the largest community in the National Park, but it is the small towns on the fringe, such as Buxton, Ashbourne, Matlock, Leek, Chapel en le Frith and Glossop, that act as major centres. Though this whole area might be encircled in a day's car tour, once you get out in the fresh air you will quickly appreciate the rich diversity of country that offers many happy years of real exploring - on foot.

## EASTERN PEAK

The eastern region of the Peak is dominated by gritstone edges that form a natural barrier between the heart of the National Park and the vast metropolis of Sheffield and Chesterfield. Running parallel far below is the River Derwent, which for the most part forms the boundary of this book and neatly complements the edges. It runs for many a long mile through villages, woodland and fields in sharp contrast to the windswept moors on which the edges rest.

The upper Derwent is special, the river born on Bleaklow's sombre moorland soon carving a deep channel through intense heather slopes. Howden and Derwent edges are collections of boulders rather than serious crags, but these important landmarks set the scene for what is to come. All too soon this moorland stream hits a premature conclusion, impounded by a chain of reservoirs: on release, above Bamford, it has lost its innocence. Perversely, Derwent's 'Lake District' is now a major attraction, though not only for its diverse scenery. Interest reaches to exploring Ladybower's 'drowned' villages at times of drought and the *Dambusters* connection, for this was the scene of wartime training runs to perfect the 'bouncing bomb' raids.

The real gritstone edges begin with Bamford Edge, overlooking the foot of Ladybower Reservoir, from where a string of craggy walls lead south by way of Stanage Edge to Birchen Edge. This unique feature has attracted rock climbers since the sport began, and today this abrasive rock offers just as much appeal, indeed greater challenges as ever more improbable routes are conquered. The valley floor supports a number of attractive villages, and from Bamford to Rowsley all repay a closer look. The former sees the Derwent swelled by the river Noe, from Edale, and at Rowsley it absorbs the river Wye from Bakewell.

Where the edges start to fade and the villages change character, the landscape subtly alters to embrace the stunning grandeur that is Chatsworth. The river puts on its Sunday best to flow sedately through exquisite parkland grazed by deer, while at the centre of things the treasure house itself stands in unparalleled splendour. Here is proof that man can sometimes improve on nature.... when nature consents.

So, whilst the Eastern Edges may dominate this area, there are walks of every flavour within these pages, and each one offers a few hours that will be long remembered.

### *Access*

Just a few decades ago, the high moors of the Peak were in the front line of the struggle for our present day freedoms. Progress was successful due to the heroic campaigns of the early ramblers; being on the doorsteps of towns and cities, the accessibility of this fine playground was the catalyst for action. Access agreements negotiated by the Peak Park have opened up great tracts - around 80 square miles - of country, and subject to a few days' closure at times of shooting, and possibly at times of high fire risk, this land is very nearly ours. In addition, walkers are almost universally welcome in the large areas of countryside in the hands of the National Trust. Sadly, east of the Derwent watershed, vast moors above Sheffield currently remain out of bounds.

In the Eastern moors, a whole array of access arrangements are in place. The Upper Derwent is overlooked by the National Trust's extensive Derwent Estate. The National Park's own Eastern Moors Estate covers a large area and further access agreements cover many of the edges and moorlands, while at the southern limits the Chatsworth Estate also welcomes walkers. Most of these areas are clearly marked on the 1:25,000 Outdoor Leisure maps (see overleaf).

Though there are various rights of way over the moors - many followed in this book - a number of the walks take advantage of the access agreements to earn more rewarding explorations. These walks gain and depart access areas at designated entry points (marked 'Boundary of Open Country' on signs). These are by way of either public or permissive paths. References to *Open Country* in the text specifically mean Access Land, rather than open countryside generally. Please adhere to these requirements, as well as observing the other by-laws. Please also remember to obey legitimate signs encountered on your walks: rights of way can be opened, closed or diverted. On these occasions official notices take precedence over the guidebook.

Finally, please take extra care to respect the life and work of the Peak. Its very accessibility puts it in the firing line when we all want to escape into the country at the same time. If we take nothing more than photographs and leave only the slightest of footprints, then this wonderful landscape will be in good shape for the next generation. In particular, ensure that dogs are kept on leads and that gates are closed behind you: probably the worst thing walkers can do is cause unnecessary headaches and expense to farmers.

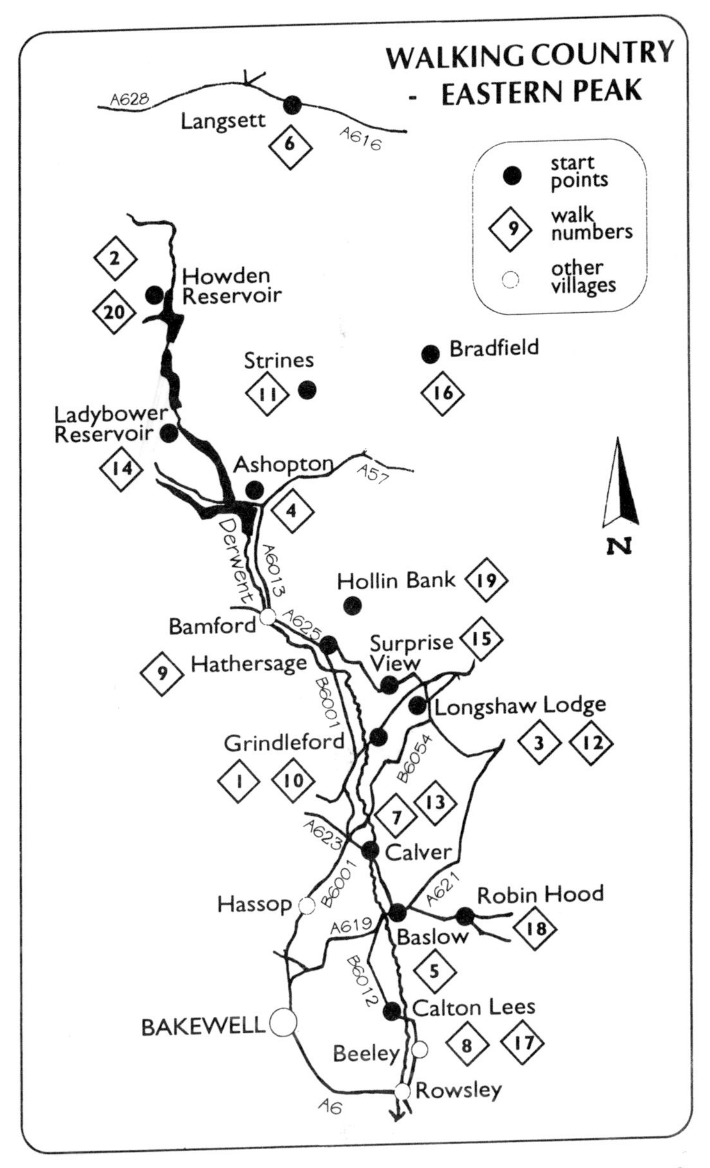
WALKING COUNTRY
- EASTERN PEAK
start points
walk numbers
other villages
A628
A616
Langsett
6
2
Howden Reservoir
20
Strines
11
Bradfield
16
Ladybower Reservoir
14
Ashopton
A57
4
Derwent
A6013
Hollin Bank
19
Bamford
A625
Surprise View
15
Hathersage
9
B6001
Longshaw Lodge
3
12
Grindleford
B6054
1
10
7
13
A623
Calver
B6001
Hassop
A621
Robin Hood
A619
Baslow
18
5
B6012
Calton Lees
BAKEWELL
8
17
Beeley
Rowsley
A6
N

***Getting around***
The area is easily reached by road from anywhere in the Peak, and from Sheffield and the M1 motorway. The Sheffield-Manchester (Hope Valley) railway is a direct route into the heart of things, with stations at Grindleford, Hathersage, Bamford, Hope and Edale. An obvious centre as a base for these walks is Hathersage, though Bakewell and Castleton are also well placed. Public transport through the area is good, for in addition to the railway most villages have a bus service, thanks in part to the proximity of Sheffield and Chesterfield.

Numerous seasonal bus services operate on less regular routes, and worthy of special mention are those serving the Upper Derwent Valley: additionally, when the road beyond Fairholmes visitor centre is closed a minibus runs to the road-end at Howden Reservoir. With a little planning, various permutations can be created by linking different sections of the walks, to create longer routes or to take advantage of public transport. Most of the starting points have some public transport, and such facilities are indicated, along with other useful information, at the start of each walk.

***Using the guide***
Each walk is self-contained, with essential information being followed by a simple map and concise description of the route. Dovetailed between this are useful notes of features along the way, and interspersed are illustrations which both capture the flavour of the walks and record the many items of interest. In order to make the instructions easier to follow, essential route description has been highlighted in bold type, while items in lighter type refer to historical asides and things to look out for: in this format you can find your way more easily while still locating features of interest at the relevant point in the text.

The simple sketch maps identify the location of the routes rather than the fine detail, and whilst the route description should be sufficient to guide you around, an Ordnance Survey map is recommended: the route can easily be plotted on the relevant OS map. To gain the most from a walk, the detail of the 1:25,000 maps is unsurpassed. They also serve to vary walks as desired, giving an improved picture of one's surroundings and the availability of linking paths. Only two Outdoor Leisure sheets are needed for complete coverage of the walks:-
•*1 - Peak District, Dark Peak* •*24 - Peak District, White Peak*

Additionally, ideal for general planning purposes are the Landranger maps at 1:50,000, and again, two cover the area:
*110 - Sheffield & Huddersfield 119 - Buxton, Matlock & Dovedale*

## SOME USEFUL ADDRESSES

**Ramblers' Association** 1/5 Wandsworth Road, London SW8 2XX
Tel. 0171-582 6878

**Peak National Park Office**
Aldern House, Baslow Road, Bakewell DE45 1AE Tel. 01629-814321

**Bakewell Visitor Centre** Tel. 01629-813227

**Castleton Visitor Centre** Tel. 01433-620679 (weekends in winter)

**Fairholmes Visitor Centre** Tel. 01433-650953 (weekends in winter)

**Langsett Barn Visitor Centre** Tel. 01226-370770
(weekends only, and limited winter Sundays)

***Tourist Information***
Peacock Information Centre, Low Pavement **Chesterfield** S40 1PB
Tel. 01246-207777/20778
The Pavilion **Matlock Bath** DE4 3NR Tel. 01629-55082
Peace Gardens **Sheffield** Tel. 0114-273 4671
Railway Station Concourse **Sheffield** Tel. 0114-279 5901

**Peak & Northern Footpaths Society**
Mr E Sutton, 1 Crossfield Grove, Marple Bridge, Cheshire SK6 5EQ
Tel. 0161-427 3582

**Friends of National Parks**
Council for National Parks, 246 Lavender Hill, London SW11 1LJ
Tel. 0171-924 4077

**Derbyshire Wildlife Trust** Elvaston Castle, Derby DE7 3ET
Tel. 01332-756610

**Yorkshire Wildlife Trust**
10 Toft Green, York YO1 1JT Tel. 01904-659570

**The National Trust** High Peak Estate Office
Edale End, Edale Rd, Hope, via Sheffield S30 2RF Tel. 01433-70368

**Bus enquiries:** 01246-250450; **Train enquiries:** 0161-832 8353

# 1

# FROGGATT EDGE

***START*** *Grindleford* *Grid ref. SK 250788*

***DISTANCE*** *5½ miles*

***ORDNANCE SURVEY MAPS***
*1:50,000*
*Landranger 119 - Buxton, Matlock & Dove Dale*
*1:25,000*
*Outdoor Leisure 24 - Peak District, White Peak*

***ACCESS*** *Start from the railway station (Sheffield-Manchester line), off the B6521 at Upper Padley above Grindleford village. Ample car parking also. Served by bus from Bakewell, Buxton and Sheffield. An alternative start is the National Trust's Haywood car park near the Grouse Inn on the B6054.*

Froggatt is one of the Peak's more famous gritstone edges, and this route takes an absorbing, circuitous approach via an historic chapel, paved ways, woodland and Froggatt village: a lovely build-up to a splendid moment as the edge is finally gained.

**S** **Leave the station by the private road over the railway.** On the right, the line disappears into the dark, gaping hole of Totley Tunnel, completed in 1893. At 6230 yards (over 3½ miles), this is the second longest rail tunnel in England, surpassed only by that beneath the Severn. **The rough road runs on past restored Padley Mill and some housing to reach Padley Chapel, opposite Brunts Barn.** This National Park ranger briefing/conservation volunteer centre was named after Harry Brunt MBE, Deputy National Park Officer who died in 1980.

Padley Chapel was restored to its impressive present condition in 1933 after long years of neglect when it served as a farm building. It is all that survives from the 15th century Padley Hall, other than the scant remains behind the chapel. The hall was home of the Roman Catholic Fitzherbert family, who came to grief in 1588 when two priests were arrested here after celebrating mass, and subsequently martyred at Derby. The chapel, with its beautiful stained glass, is open to view on Sunday and Wednesday afternoons, April-September, and a remembrance service is held on the Thursday nearest July 12th.

**Over the cattle-grid just beyond, take a gate on the left to cross the railway by a high stone bridge, with the signal box just down to the left. Descending the field beyond, leave the track before the trees, passing through a gateway for a slim path to cross to the far corner. Go left with the wall, curving gently down and a path forming as bracken is entered. In the very corner the Derwent is briefly glimpsed at a farm bridge over a side stream.**

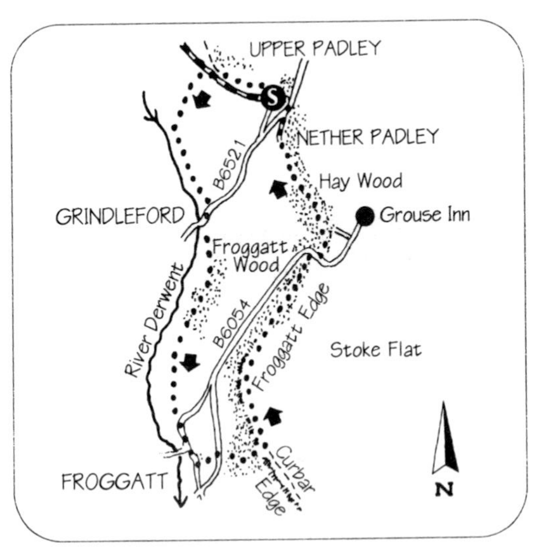


The stream is Burbage Brook, in its final few yards after a short but lively existence from the heather moors down through the Longshaw estate and the wooded delights of Padley Gorge. **Go left over the bridge and a fieldside path heads away, not joining the river until the final stretch onto the road at Grindleford Bridge.** Over this last stage the views ahead to the Froggatt skyline find the true edge largely masked by the trees immediately beneath it.

**Go right and cross to a kissing-gate opposite, just before the bridge.** To the left is St. Helen's church, while the attractive house across the road is the former tollhouse, with an Ordnance Survey benchmark plate at the base of its wall. Just over the bridge is Grindleford village with several shops and a gallery. The old smithy can be seen opposite the Post office, while the flagged way alongside will lead to the pub, the *Sir William*.

**A 1905 Peak and Northern Footpaths Society guidepost sends us through the kissing-gate onto a field path. At the end pass through a kissing-gate and go right along the fieldside to enter the extensive Froggatt Wood. Remain on the main path running on near the wood bottom.** Features en route include an attractive glade where a stream forms a small pool; a large boulder with three mysterious carved slots; and some sections of paved path.

*Padley Chapel*

**Emerging at the end, cross the field to a gateway, noting further sections of paving. Swing right in front of a barn and then left again at a wall corner, some kerbing sending the path along to become enclosed. This is Spooner Lane, a paved central section leading virtually all the way to a junction in sleepy Froggatt.**

In front is the Wesleyan Reform chapel, with some attractive cottages around. **Go straight ahead, making use of the raised walkway to run on to a T-junction alongside Froggatt Bridge. Don't cross but keep straight on Froggatt Lane, and within a couple of minutes take a stile on the left between gardens. A good path climbs the open pasture through an assortment of scrub to emerge onto the B6054 again in higher Froggatt.** Those seeking refreshment will find the *Chequers Inn* handily placed just along to the left.

*Froggatt Bridge*

**Across the road a path climbs through woodland, entering Open Country at a stile part way. Going straight over a cross-path continue up through the beautiful woodland, breaking out only at the very base of the cliffs of Froggatt Edge.** First feature of note is the impressive bulk of the detached Froggatt Pinnacle just along to the left. Scramblers might seek a bolder route onto the edge, perhaps using the gap at the rear of the pinnacle. **The path swings right to an obvious break to clamber up onto the crest.** This makes a super spot to recover and most likely watch climbers in action, for Froggatt is one of the Peak's more revered climbing edges.

**Turn left to follow a broad path along the crest of Froggatt Edge.** Savour now the superb valley views, while to the right the moorland of Stoke Flat sits beneath the higher level White Edge. Breaks to peer over the edges are the norm, though be careful and don't frighten the climbers. **Shortly a branch path goes to investigate the stone circle just yards off the path.** This modest affair consists of a number of small stones almost swamped in the bracken, and is thought to date from the Bronze age, perhaps 4000 or 5000 years ago.

**Beyond the circle some outcrops offer further good valley views before the main path runs on into silver birch woodland, ultimately emerging alongside a large boulder.** A little scramble to its crest earns a fine panorama over the Derwent Valley with Win Hill and Stanage Edge prominent. **The path swings round to join the B6054.**

**Go right a few yards and cross with caution to a small gate. A path descends into the National Trust's Haywood, running on colourfully beyond a stream to reach a car park. Our path keeps left of it to drop to a bridle-gate to slant down through Hay Wood. After briefly running level the main path drops away again, but here keep straight on the more inviting green path. This ultimately drops a little to reach a kissing-gate out of the wood. A snicket runs on above the select housing of Nether Padley to join their drive (Tedgness Road). Turn right on this to meet the B6521. Go right a few yards then down an urbanised path through trees to return to Grindleford station.**

*Froggatt Pinnacle*

2

# HOWDEN EDGE

***START*** *Howden Reservoir* *Grid ref. SK 167938*

***DISTANCE*** *7½ miles*

***ORDNANCE SURVEY MAPS***
*1:50,000*
*Landranger 110 - Sheffield & Huddersfield*
*1:25,000*
*Outdoor Leisure 1 - Peak District, Dark Peak*

***ACCESS*** *Start from the King's Tree parking area at the Upper Derwent Valley road end. On Summer weekends/BH Mondays the road is closed, but is accessible by a regular bus service from Fairholmes visitor centre. Virtually the whole walk is within the National Trust's Derwent estate, where walkers enjoy open access subject to by-laws.*

A splendid ramble featuring deep cloughs and spacious moorland edges, and visiting the highest points in South Yorkshire.

**Ⓢ For the opening section to Slippery Stones please refer to the opening paragraph on page 90 (WALK 20), with which it coincides. Open country beckons, so cross the bridge to leave the trees and crowds behind. Take the path upstream, quickly reaching a bridleway junction at a guidepost. Double back right along the broad path.** This is a favourite with family bikers undertaking a straightforward reservoir circuit.

**The track runs an undulating course down the valley, first around the moorland flank of Cold Side then along the edge of the plantations with Howden Reservoir just below.** It is a touch disconcerting to observe the car park just five minutes away across the reservoir! **After a mile or so we commence a large loop to swing in to cross the bottom of Howden Clough.**

**Just beyond a hairpin, leave the broad track and double sharply back along a pleasant footpath into the plantation. This soon emerges into open country to cross a tiny stream.** Our path can be seen ahead, rising up the flank of the clough. **A thin path resumes upstream, rising above a small dam. At the end of it, ignore the path straight ahead and bear left up the rising path.** This splendid old way, made to link with the Cut Gate, rises effortlessly out of the clough. **At the top it swings left and commences a much gentler rise, part level, with the higher ground now opening out.**

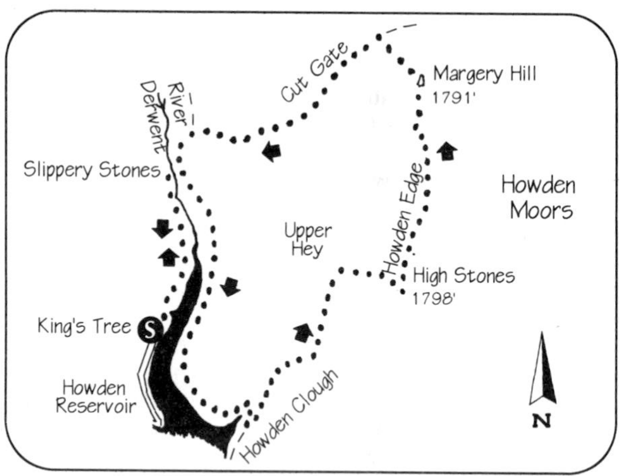


Straight ahead are the High Stones on Howden Edge, our objective. Back over to the right are the bouldery environs of Back Tor (WALKS 11 and 14 visit Back Tor). **The thin path remains infallible as it levels out on the broad col of Upper Hey. When it starts to falter, break off right through tussocky grassy before climbing steeper but far more inviting ground to gain the rocky edge of High Stones.**

A cairn sits back from the edge, marking the summit of our walk (just) at 1798ft/548m. It is also the highest point in South Yorkshire. Sitting atop the buttress there is much to survey: we are looking down into Howden and Cranberry Cloughs, with the heather-clad Derwent moors around to the north enclosing the wild upper reaches of the Derwent Valley. Immediately to the north the modest but neat edge is an inviting prospect for our next mile, running along to the white Ordnance Survey column on Margery Hill, and indeed many miles beyond for those intent on a major leg-stretcher.

**Now simply head north along the edge, a clear path passing above numerous scattered outcrops.** Some of these are of a particularly gnarled gritstone, splendid foregrounds for the views down to the dam of Howden Reservoir. **An easy, near level march leads all the way along to meet the Cut Gate path, but on approaching Margery Hill it is traditional to take a branch trod slanting across to the Ordnance Survey column (2965 - note the absence of the usual 'S' prefix).** At 1791ft/546m this popular landmark is a mere handful of feet lower than the less well known High Stones. It sits in a peaty hollow surrounded by stones, but is surely not on the highest ground. All-round views include a windfarm in front of the Emley Moor TV mast.

**Either rejoin the edge path below or forge straight on north to quickly intercept the Cut Gate path.** The Cut Gate is an old way linking the Derwent Valley with the outside world at the *Flouch Inn*. When the upper Derwent was farmed as a living community this was the direct way to civilisation - and market at Penistone.

**Turn left along this, quickly descending the moor on a flagged path, then becoming delectably grassy.** Curving round above Bull Clough it provides a delightful spell looking into its deep confines with the Bull Stones proudly on the skyline; the addition of the walk's first heather carpet is a worthy bonus. **Running back along to the left the path encounters a steep section, recently stepped to halt erosion and ease progress (other than for bikers!). At the bottom Bull Clough's tiny stream is crossed and a level path runs out to the main valley, quickly joining its path. Turn left for two minutes to return to the bridge at Slippery Stones, then retrace the opening mile.**

*The old packhorse bridge at Slippery Stones*

# 3

# WHITE EDGE MOOR

***START*** *Longshaw Lodge* *Grid ref. SK 266800*

***DISTANCE*** *4½ miles*

***ORDNANCE SURVEY MAPS***
*1:50,000*
*Landranger 119 - Buxton, Matlock & Dove Dale*
*1:25,000*
*Outdoor Leisure 24 - Peak District, White Peak*

***ACCESS*** *Start from the National Trust car park at Longshaw Lodge, on the B6055 just off the A625 at the Fox House Inn. Sheffield-Bakewell and Sheffield-Buxton buses pass the car park entrance.*
*• ACCESS AREA -* *see page 8.*

An easy upland stroll embracing fine views and a wealth of features; parkland, moorland, woodland, an ancient cross, a hint of a gritstone edge and even a well placed pub.

**S A path runs from the bottom of the car park into trees and down over a stone arched bridge to a junction behind the house: the visitor centre is just round the front.**

Longshaw Lodge was built in the 19th century and served as a salubrious shooting lodge for the Dukes of Rutland, when the shooting scene was in its heyday in terms of both grouse bags and social occasions. When the estate was sold off in the 1930s the National Trust acquired a portion, while the house itself was ultimately converted into apartments. The National Trust estate is run as a country park, and alongside the lodge is a visitor centre with information, shop, restaurant and toilets. It is normally open Wednesday to Sunday, late March to Christmas. The car park is open daily. Each September major sheepdog trials are held here.

**From the front of the lodge head back up the drive towards the car park, but remain on the main track which runs up behind the house and on through the trees. It rises to a gate out of the wood, then runs right as a fine green way through open country.** At once there are views over the estate and the Derwent Valley to Eyam Moor and higher country towards Edale and Kinder Scout. Features en route are Little John's Well, a spring dribbling into a stone trough beneath the drive; and just past that a stone stairway climbing the colourful bank.

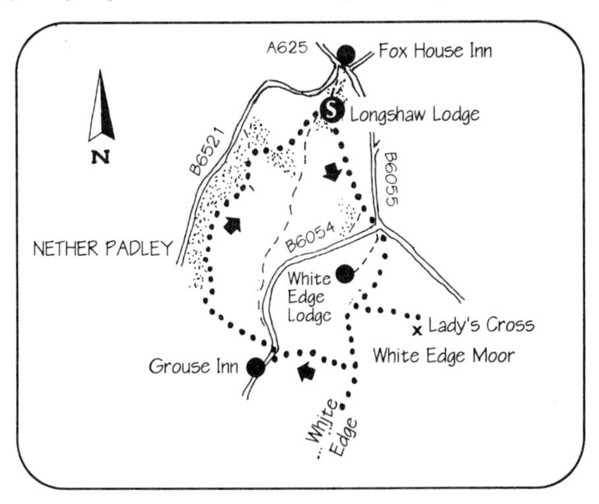


**At a fork bear left to rise to a gate onto the B6055 at Wooden Pole. The pole stands proud on the left just before the gate. Go right and across the triangle at the junction. Ignore the National Trust sign in favour of an Open Country sign to its left. From the stile a part waymarked path rises with a fence onto a brow on White Edge Moor.** The sweeping moors of Totley Moss roll away to the left. **Remain with the path to another brow above a pair of small plantations, then cross the moor to a notice at a fence-stile above White Edge Lodge.**

At 1273ft/388m this is the summit of the walk, with views ahead to the greater length of the lower level White Edge. **An interesting detour takes the footpath to the left to see Lady's Cross. It's no more than a pleasant ten minutes through the heather, dropping gently down before espying the cross 50 yards over to the right.** Its stumpy shaft stands firmly in a base with the year 1618 inscribed, on the site of a medieval crossroads (Hope-Chesterfield and Sheffield-Tideswell).

**Back at the notice and path crossroads, resume south on the broad path (with Barbrook Reservoir in view over to the left), striking across White Edge Moor to reach a gateway in an old wall. This is another turning point, but with White Edge outstretched ahead, the best advice is to go on for a few minutes, at least to the first outcrops encountered.** These make an ideal location to break out the sandwiches. The edge continues for a couple of miles, well defined but of occasional boulders rather than noteworthy crags. If so inclined, one could go all the way, dropping down to Curbar Gap and returning along Curbar and Froggatt edges: an excellent expedition that is a true 'edges' walk.

**Back at the gateway take the path down the near side, dropping through heather to join up with a bridleway. Turn down this, through scattered native woodland to a gate (end of Open Country) before running across a pasture to the B6054 by the *Grouse Inn*. Go right along the road (after a few yards' detour?) and at the bend take a stile opposite. A broad green track heads away, down the rough pasture between wall and stream.**

There are good views ahead over Padley Gorge to the well wooded valley floor with Win Hill backed by the Mam Tor ridge and Kinder Scout, and also Bamford Edge leading up to Stanage Edge and the distinctive features of Hathersage Moor (Higger Tor is seen rising with superiority above Carl Wark). **Further down err nearer the stream to descend better defined as the way narrows approaching a wood.**

*Lady's Cross*

Cross the stream near the bottom and contour right past the wall corner, using a short paved section to reach a tiny sidestream. Here the main path drops sharply left into the wood. Instead, take the sunken path rising away, up through this colourful corner to the wood top. Keep on to meet a firmer path, bearing left with a parallel wall. Keep on past a gate to find a stile 100 yards further in the very wall corner. Just beyond it our path meets a broader one climbing from the left.

*The Grouse Inn, Longshaw*

Turn right along this, enjoying some cracking views over the environs of Grindleford station in the valley far below, and also across to the various rock architecture of Hathersage Moor. At a gate at the end the wall turns away to leave us in no-man's-land. Take the path straight on, running pleasantly through open terrain with woodland either side. Keep left at a couple of minor stream crossings, after the second one rising imperceptibly left onto a broader track.

As the track levels out approaching Granby Wood, take a green path swinging right to rise up to the edge of a pond. Here a firm path rises right, soon becoming enclosed by rhododendrons and a ditch. At the top take the left-hand gate and the path runs on above Longshaw Meadow, beneath the lodge's ha-ha and out to the front of the house. There are more fine views across to Hathersage Moor to finish.

4

# WHINSTONE LEE TOR

***START*** *Ashopton* *Grid ref. SK 195864*

***DISTANCE*** *5½ miles*

***ORDNANCE SURVEY MAPS***
*1:50,000*
*Landranger 110 - Sheffield & Huddersfield*
*1:25,000*
*Outdoor Leisure 1 - Peak District, Dark Peak*

***ACCESS*** *Start from the eastern end of Ashopton Viaduct on Ladybower Reservoir. There is a lengthy parking area alongside the A57 overlooking the reservoir. Ashopton is served by Sheffield-Castleton buses, while Summer Sunday/BH Monday buses from Manchester, Rochdale, Sheffield and Matlock all use the Snake Pass between Glossop and Ladybower.*

Easy walking by reservoir, woodland and moorland, with a fine selection of views over the Ladybower environs of the Derwent Valley.

(S) Ladybower Reservoir was completed in 1945, third and final of the Upper Derwent's reservoirs. Unfortunately the village of Ashopton was sacrificed along with that of Derwent, further up the valley (see WALK 14). This artificial lakeland may be deemed to have a certain attractive merit, and indeed is quite a tourist draw, but one glimpse at photographs of the once green valley around Ashopton is enough to realise what loveliness was annihilated.

Ashopton consisted of numerous farms and cottages, a pub, the *Ashopton Inn*, chapel and other useful facilities for travellers on the former turnpike road. It now rests in the deep, just south of the viaduct, and unlike Derwent has taken all its secrets with it.

**Cross the road at the start of the Ashopton Viaduct, but not the viaduct itself. A private road heads along the reservoir side, but as it quickly doubles back up to the right keep straight on the rough road through the gate ahead. This runs on above the reservoir shore.** An early glimpse of the viaduct finds it overlooked by Win Hill's oft dark shadow, while as the trees recede there are fine views up the reservoir. When water levels are low it is possible to discern some remains of Derwent village.

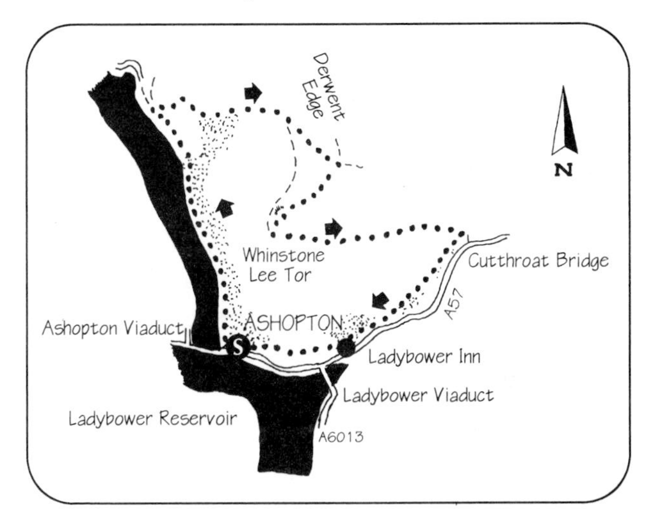


**After about 1½ miles leave this road, immediately through a gate with a hairpin farm road in front. Don't follow this, but take a gate on the right (footpath to Moscar). A steep path climbs the field then swings right at the top.** At this point our objective of Whinstone Lee Tor is prominent at the end of the skyline ridge. **The path turns to climb again to a group of barns.** Note the lintel on the first barn, dated 1647. **Beyond them the path swings right to cross Grindle Clough, then rises away with a wall, slanting above a plantation to emerge onto rough moor-like pasture.** Up ahead are the weird rock sculptures of White Tor and the Wheel Stones.

**A steady path slants across the pasture up to a gate onto open heather moor.** If not having already surveyed the view, then pause to look back to the Mam Tor ridge and the great girth of Kinder Scout. **Go**

**right a mere hundred yards from the gate then leave the bridleway by an initially thin path slanting up to the left at a guidepost. It is marked by cairns in an effort to re-assert itself, as over the years it has been usurped by an imposter which sets off from a little further along the track.** Sections of paving have recently been uncovered on the old path, with possibly more waiting to be unearthed. **The way slants up through the bracken, merging into the broader path to rise onto the heathery edge, where a guidepost presides over a cross-roads of paths.**

*Ashopton Viaduct and Win Hill*

**Turn right along the edge.** This brief section along the ridge via Whinstone Lee Tor to the Moscar bridleway is neither right of way nor access land, but a long established path that has enjoyed common usage over many decades: please don't stray onto the open moor to the east. Almost at once, on a slight knoll, look back to see the Wheel Stones just further back up the ridge, backed by White Tor and even distant Back Tor slotting in between the two. **Our fine skyline walk leads down the edge to Whinstone Lee Tor, passing the Hurkling Stones en route.**

The jumble of boulders offers an ideal place to repose, an airy vantage overlooking a vast stretch of Ladybower Reservoir. Back up along Derwent Edge are the Wheel Stones and White Tor, while across Ladybower are the Bleaklow moors leading around to Kinder Scout, with Grindslow Knoll pointing skywards. Rushup Edge, Lose Hill and Mam Tor lead the way round to Win Hill, the Ashopton Viaduct and Ladybower's western arm; while the branches of little known Grainfoot Clough, immediately beneath our knoll, are worth more than a passing glance. Affixed to a rock is a small memorial plaque to a Sheffield rambler.

**Resume on the path descending steeply to a junction of ways where we rejoin the Derwent-Moscar bridleway. Turn left along it for a very gentle stroll across the moor, descending steadily through the heather before dropping down to a clough just above the A57 at Cutthroat Bridge. At a crossroads of green ways the main track drops down to join the road, but our return route curves right (through an area blackened after a recent moorland fire), picking up a branch from below to set off back west. This is a splendid level amble through bracken and heather, spoiled only by intrusive overhead wires.**

**At a gate we enter Ladybower Wood, a nature reserve of the Derbyshire Wildlife Trust. The scattered native woodland is a delight as the path forges on before commencing a more pronounced drop. Shortly after leaving the reserve the road is seen just below. The track drops down to it, rather handily alongside the *Ladybower Inn*.** A return along the road/reservoir side is possible from here, but a better option awaits.

**Just short of the road (or indeed after a pint) a less obvious path branches right off the track. This initially thin path contours off through bracken, broadening as it rises through woodland. Emerging, it rises further in the company of a tall wall beneath a bracken bank before levelling off.** As the wall drops away enjoy superb views over the lower section of Ladybower Reservoir and along its western arm. Bamford Edge projects itself high above the Ladybower Viaduct. **The path then drops down through tall bracken to join a forest road. Go down this to pass the few dwellings of Ashopton and emerge back at the start.**

# 5

# CHATSWORTH

***START*** *Baslow* *Grid ref. SK 258721*

***DISTANCE*** *6 miles*

***ORDNANCE SURVEY MAPS***
*1:50,000*
*Landranger 119 - Buxton, Matlock & Dove Dale*
*1:25,000*
*Outdoor Leisure 24 - Peak District, White Peak*

***ACCESS*** *Start from the car park in the village centre. Served by bus from Chesterfield, Bakewell, Matlock, Buxton, Sheffield and Leek, and many other places in between.*

A splendid ramble around the prestigious grounds of Chatsworth House. Polish your boots before setting off! The return leg is on concession paths courtesy of the estate.

**S** Baslow is a well-to-do village on the edge of the Chatsworth estate, disjointed by the main road through it. It is in fact a collection of settlements such as Nether End, Bridge End, West End and Over End. Outside the car park is a small green (Goose Green) overlooked by the obligàtory *Devonshire Arms*, and just along the road is another pub, the *Wheatsheaf*, while there are several shops and cafes.

Bridge End is dominated by St. Anne's church in spacious environs, its steeple typical of the area. Though restored in the 19th century, the tower has survived over 700 years. The bridge itself is a beautiful, high-arched 400 year old structure, with a very simple one-man tollbooth still in place. Outside the church are two further pubs, the *Prince of Wales* and the *Rutland Arms*. The latter reminds us of the proximity of the estates of the Duke of Rutland of nearby Haddon Hall. Indeed, the Haddon estate owned the Baslow end of Chatsworth until a trade of land in 1823.

**From Goose Green go right on the short-lived street past lovely cottages at Nether End.** Pause on the bridge over Bar Brook to admire the chocolate box scene across it. **Turn right along the little road along the front of the thatched cottages. Pass through a stile by the gate at the end and a footpath runs on past a lodge-type estate house (an Ordnance Survey benchmark plate is affixed to the bottom corner) to enter Chatsworth Park via a kissing-gate.** A notice advises that all the open parkland ahead is free to wander, though for the record our route through to One Arch Bridge is a public right of way.

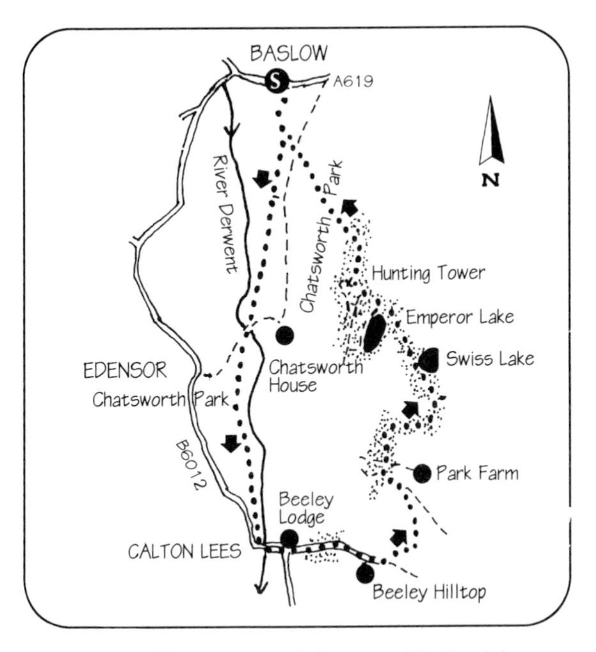


Chatsworth is one of the great stately houses of England, known as the 'Palace of the Peak'. It is the seat of the Cavendish family headed by the Duke of Devonshire. The original house was started in 1562 by Bess of Hardwick (Countess of Shrewsbury) who married Sir William Cavendish. His son became the first Earl of Devonshire in 1618, the fourth Earl became the first Duke in 1694, and the line continues to this day. The present house dates from 1686-1707 when the first Duke decided to start afresh on exactly the same site. The north wing was added a century later.

During the 19th century the 6th Duke engaged Sir Thomas Paxton who largely created the present gardens including the Emperor Fountain, and also Edensor village (after the original was demolished after being deemed too near the house). Despite being the Duke's right-hand man on the estate he also found time to design the Crystal Palace in 1861. The impressive stable block behind the house was designed by James Paine in 1758-64. Chatsworth is open to the public who may cast their eyes on a treasure house filled with riches galore. Alternatively the thought of all this in the hands of one family may turn you off completely, but even then, you can't fail to be impressed!

*Cottages at Nether End, Baslow*

**Head off on the broad path in front through archetypal English parkland, picking up Home Farm drive and going on past the little White Lodge.** These spacious grounds were laid out by the celebrated landscape architect Lancelot 'Capability' Brown in the 1760s on behalf of the 4th Duke. High to the left the Hunting Tower stands above the trees, we shall be stood alongside it near the end of the walk. **Ahead, meanwhile, the house itself is revealed. Ignoring branches keep straight on this direct line, passing the cricket ground to arrive at Queen Mary's Bower.** After the cricket ground one could make directly for the riverbank, if desired.

Queen Mary's Bower is one of those curiosities that adorn the English countryside. It is so named as the captive Mary, Queen of Scots found relaxation in her small garden here during spells at Chatsworth in the 1570s. Along with the Hunting Tower on the skyline, it is all that remains of Bess of Hardwick's original works at Chatsworth. It was restored about 1830 and is thought to include an ancient earthwork guarding a ford on the Derwent.

**Behind the Bower join the main drive to cross Chatsworth Bridge.** This elegant structure was designed by James Paine in 1761. **Once across turn left to wander through open parkland again with the river for divine company.** Initially it forms a perfect foreground to the house. **Simply remain by the river, past a shell of a building to a kissing-gate onto the road at One Arch (or Blue) Bridge.** The curious architecture of the ruin (illustrated on page 42) belies its history as a mill: it dates from 1760 and until 1952 it ground corn for animal feeds, then stood redundant for ten years before succumbing to three giant beeches that collapsed onto it during a gale. The bridge was another designed by James Paine, in 1760.

**Cross the bridge and go along to Beeley Lodge on the bend. Here turn up a road alongside. This climbs steeply past woods and to Beeley Hilltop.** In the early stages there are views left into the park, where fallow deer may be spotted. Beeley Hilltop is an imposing early 18th century house. **Here the road becomes a rough byway, and just beyond the barns leave it by a stile on the left.** From here back to the Baslow park entrance we are on concession paths.

**Rise up the field to a stile at a gate to enter the dense bracken flank of the Rabbit Warren. A good path rises left to gain the distinct edge.** This marks the end of the climbing and is a fine place to linger: better still go right for two minutes along the track and break journey on the modest outcrops.

**Resuming, go left along the firm track to enter the wooded grounds. The drive swings right to a crossroads with the Park Farm drive. Cross straight over and the broad track swings right then left to run on past the attractive Swiss Lake.** Across the water is the isolated Swiss Cottage, dating from 1839. **The track then swings left to the head of Emperor Lake.** This extensive pond was created by Thomas Paxton to supply the Emperor Fountain. **Here the main track swings round to the right to run on to the Hunting Tower.**

During summer when the house is open there may be others here, for a direct path climbs from the house. It certainly marks a fine viewpoint with the broad break offering views over the park and across the river to Edensor, with its spire dominating all. The tower itself is also known as the Stand Tower and (along with Queen Mary's Bower) is the sole legacy of Bess of Hardwick's 16th century work. It was used by the ladies to observe the progress of the hunt, and today is a private house.

**Just beyond, the track joins a surfaced one climbing from the left. Advance straight on this for five minutes, then take a signposted footpath down through the trees. It emerges into the open park at a stile above a ditch and bank.** There is a good chance of observing more fallow deer in this quieter part well away from the house. **Maintain the slant down over a broad track and then a surfaced estate road. Continue across to pick up the outward path by the pedestrian entrance, and retrace the walk's opening five minutes.**

*The Hunting Tower*

# 6

# MIDHOPE MOORS

***START*** *Langsett* *Grid ref. SE 210004*

***DISTANCE*** *5 miles*

***ORDNANCE SURVEY MAPS***
*1:50,000*
*Landranger 110 - Sheffield & Huddersfield*
*1:25,000*
*Outdoor Leisure 1 - Peak District, Dark Peak*

***ACCESS*** *Start from the Yorkshire Water car park at Langsett Barn, on the A616. Served by Barnsley/Penistone-Stocksbridge buses.*

An easy circuit of Langsett Reservoir, improved greatly by an extension loop on good moorland paths. The direct walk omitting this is just 4 miles.

**S** Langsett is a small community on the north-eastern corner of the Peakland moors, though it is linked firmly to the more populated nearby areas of South Yorkshire than the National Park. It supports a youth hostel, cafe/shop and the *Waggon & Horses* pub with a Victorian postbox on its wall. Langsett Barn was restored in 1993 and features a 1621 initialled datestone and a superb roof structure that is sufficient reason to enter within. It operates as a National Park Visitor Centre, toilets, ranger base, and local community centre.

**From the car park a path runs left of the barn to join the main road. Go right past the pub and turn along the Strines/Derwent Valley road. This runs along the dam wall of Langsett Reservoir.** Built in the 1890s it is the largest reservoir serving Sheffield, with a capacity of 1408 million gallons. The castellated tower is said to be a replica of a tower at Lancaster Castle. In view across it, beyond the obligatory plantations, are the heather moors we shall soon be tramping.

**At the end the road winds round past trees, and here leave it by an enclosed bridlepath (Thickwoods Lane) on the right. Reaching a fork take the footpath bearing right off it, running an embowered course through to the edge of Upper Midhope. Go briefly left on the concrete road then turn down a snicket on the right.** This tiny hamlet features some attractive cottages: note also the old iron Sheffield Corporation Waterworks sign.

**The Strines road is rejoined on a hairpin bend. Turn immediately right from the parking area on a private road, and at a fork keep straight on the forest road ahead. This runs around an arm of the reservoir to emerge onto the edge of the heather moor on crossing the stream. The broad track climbs right between moor and trees.**

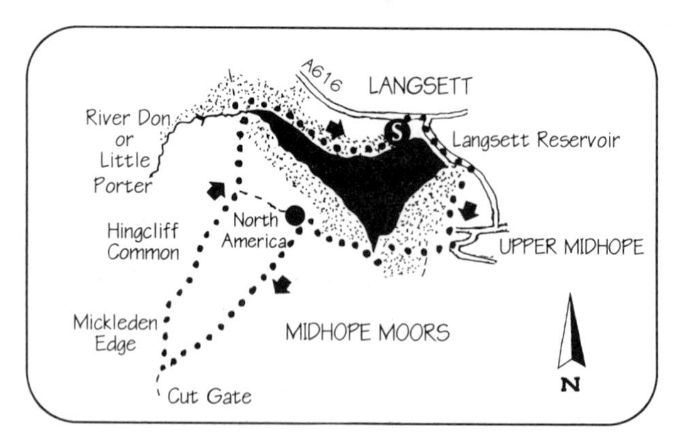


**Before long the track rises away from the trees to run on to a gate in front of the low ruins of North America, a farm sacrificed for water gathering.** Ahead on the skyline is Ingbirchworth windfarm. For the direct reservoir circuit, keep straight on the broad path past the ruins to merge into the Cut Gate a little further. **For the 'wilder' part of the walk turn up the near side of the wall, a thin path rising through heather and broadening as it absorbs a short-cut at another wall corner.**

**This same path rises gradually away: on a knoll the crumbling wall turns away and leaves us to forge on, level or gently uphill to arrive at a junction with the Cut Gate.** This is marked by an old guidepost pointing the way to numerous destinations; a novel one being

Hazlehead Station, which closed several decades ago, even before the Woodhead line was abandoned completely! Finest feature however is the sudden appearance of the colourful valley of Mickleden at our feet, a fine prospect (you'll have to assume Pike o'Stickle is in the clouds). The Cut Gate is an historic route used by the farmers of the upper Derwent Valley (before being flooded out) to reach the *Flouch Inn* crossroads and Penistone market.

*Old guidepost, Mickleden Edge*

**Turn down the path which briefly enjoys the delights of Mickleden Edge before running across the moor of Hingcliff Common. It descends to absorb the direct path, then more broadly down to the plantation edge and finally steeply to the stone arched Brook House Bridge.** Immediately upstream, still in Open Country, the bank of the Porter or Little Don River makes a grand spot for a final break.

**Across the bridge the broad track climbs away, but at the first chance take a path to the right to quickly enter the plantation. Almost at once it is sent down to the right to run along the bottom of the trees, above the reservoir wall. In time it is directed to double back up to the left, then resuming at a higher level before slanting up again to run on to merge with a higher path. Just past here it re-enters the car park at Langsett Barn.**

# CURBAR EDGE

***START*** *Calver* *Grid ref. SK 247744*

***DISTANCE*** *5 miles*

***ORDNANCE SURVEY MAPS***
*1:50,000*
*Landranger 119 - Buxton, Matlock & Dove Dale*
*1:25,000*
*Outdoor Leisure 24 - Peak District, White Peak*

***ACCESS*** *Start from the old bridge on the Derwent linking Calver and Curbar. There is reasonable parking on the old road, immediately upstream of the modern bridge on the A623. Served by bus from Sheffield, Chesterfield, Buxton, Bakewell and numerous other less frequent services. • ACCESS AREA -* *see page 8.*

An easy walk that more than most combines outstanding variety, even by the high standards set hereabouts: riverbank and woodland precede a lengthy stride along gritstone edges backed by heather seas: there's also a fair dab of history.

**S** Calver Bridge spans the Derwent at the eastern end of the village, its 18th century arches happily by-passed by the busy road. On the east bank are the village school, church and pub, the aptly named *Bridge Inn*. All Saints church dates from 1868 and is shared between Calver, Curbar and Froggatt. On the west bank are shops, a cafe and a craft centre.

**From the Calver side of the bridge a private road runs alongside the shop, and on past the old mill.** The enormous Calver Mill was built as a cotton mill in 1785 and rebuilt by Richard Arkwright in 1804 after a fire. If a member of the group wants to count the windows, then we'll see them back here in 2 or 3 hours! The mill was used for filming the

TV series *Colditz* in the 1970s, and it's a fair bet that the early millworkers viewed it as their own equivalent of Colditz! **At Stocking Farm pass to the right of the buildings and down to a kissing-gate.** Already Curbar Edge is well displayed ahead, above the woods. **A path runs on to join the Goit.** This was cut to supply water from the Derwent to the mill, originating at a weir upstream; the river is, for now, hidden just across it. **Head upstream through wooded surrounds to join the B6054 at New Bridge.** Note that an alternative path clings tightly to the opposite bank.

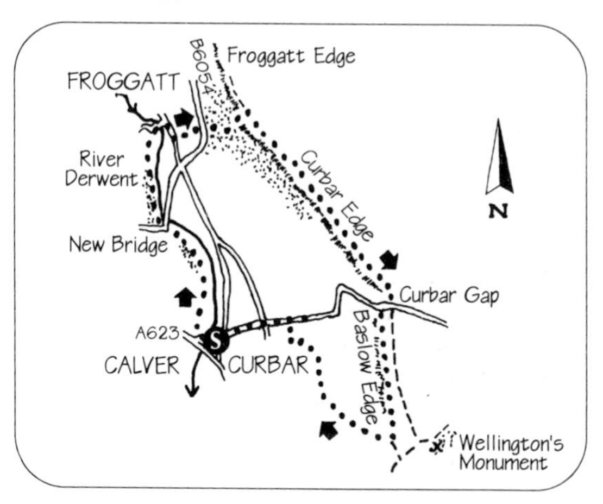


**Cross straight over the road at New Bridge and resume upstream on the riverbank proper. Our splendid path runs on past a marshy habitat of gnarled trees. At the end the path takes a stile onto the minor road at Froggatt Bridge.** This dates from the 17th century and features two very different arches (illustrated on page 15).

**Cross to a T-junction in the scattered settlement of Froggatt and go right on Froggatt Lane. After a couple of minutes take a stile on the left between gardens. A good path climbs the open pasture through an assortment of scrub to emerge onto the B6054 again in higher Froggatt.** The *Chequers Inn* is handily placed just along to the left. **Across the road a path climbs through woodland, entering Open Country at a stile part way. Going straight over a cross-path continue up through the beautiful woodland, breaking out only at the very base of the cliffs of Froggatt Edge.**

First feature of note on reaching the edge is the impressive bulk of the detached Froggatt Pinnacle just along to the left (illustrated on page 16). Scramblers might seek a bolder route onto the edge, perhaps using a gap at the rear of the pinnacle. **The path swings right to an obvious break to clamber up onto the crest.** This makes a super spot to recover and most likely watch climbers in action, for Froggatt is one of the Peak's more revered climbing edges.

*Curbar Edge, looking south to Baslow Edge*

**Turn right on the good path that faithfully traces the edge, the only change being that of name, to the higher level and more substantial Curbar Edge.** Enjoy outstanding views over the Derwent Valley, north to High Peak country, across to Eyam Moor and down the valley to further edges; at our feet are Curbar and Calver. **As the rocks abate the path drops gently down and swings left to leave the moor for the narrow road through Curbar Gap.** For a quick return turn down the road to Curbar. The car park is just along to the left and at its far end, just over a stile in the field corner, stands an old guidepost, the name *Dronfield* being best discerned.

**Crossing straight over, a path heads off again onto more open moorland. The main track is a bridleway, initially with a wall and then running free. For greater interest however take a path branch-**

**ing right to gain the start of Baslow Edge at a view indicator. Though not as dramatic as what has gone before, this is in many ways a more intimate, relaxing section traversing this colourful terrain amidst a lesser quantity of fellow humans.**

Towards the end the presence of the great boulder of the Eagle Stone over to the left may tempt a detour: one might also keep on to a path crossroads in front of the nearby Wellington's Monument (see WALK 18). If visiting the monument (illustrated on page 1), return along the rough track west/right, and as it drops gently down, a broad branch right curves round beneath quarries and along a wallside to pick up our direct route down from Baslow Edge.

**As the path swings left before an old quarry, the direct route slips down a narrower grassy trod to join the bridleway contouring beneath. Turn right as it doubles back well below the edge, dropping down by the wall through bracken. As it slants away from the wall, cross a contouring path and down to another above a wood corner. Here branch right, running on now with both Curbar and Baslow edges appearing high above. Towards the end of open ground it arrives at some old graves.** Five initialled gravestones are those of the Cundy family, struck down by plague in 1632 some decades before the more famous events at Eyam.

**From the graves the main path drops left to a stile off the moor and finally out of Open Country. A path descends the field to a stile in the opposite corner.** Before passing through, note a curious building with a stepped roof in the garden on the right. It is said to have been a lock-up for holding 18th century wrongdoers before transporting to a more secure gaol. **Beyond the stile a private drive (Lane Farm) is joined. Cross to the bridle-gate in the corner and descend a narrow snicket. Towards the bottom as it swings left near the house, find an easily missed stile in the little corner on the right. Cross the field bottom to a stile onto another narrow way. This runs on between suburban gardens to join Bar Lane.**

**Descend the lane, becoming Curbar Lane, through this scattered village.** Part way down, opposite Pinfold Lane, the old pinfold survives, where stray farm stock could be detained until returned to their owners. **With Calver Mill appearing below, the road drops steeply to emerge onto the junction alongside the church and rather neatly opposite the pub.**

# 8

# HOB HURST'S HOUSE

***START*** *Calton Lees* *Grid ref. SK 258685*

***DISTANCE*** *6½ miles*

***ORDNANCE SURVEY MAPS***
*1:50,000*
*Landranger 119 - Buxton, Matlock & Dove Dale*
*1:25,000*
*Outdoor Leisure 24 - Peak District, White Peak*

***ACCESS*** *Start from the Calton Lees car park on the B6012 south of Baslow. Served by Calver-Matlock buses, and also from Bakewell, Sheffield and Chesterfield on Summer Sundays/BH Mondays. A start from Beeley would reduce the walking to 5 miles, but there is only limited roadside parking. • Some sections are on concession paths -* *see page 8.*

A varied ramble to visit a Bronze Age burial mound high on the moors, the entire walk with strong overtones of the Chatsworth estate.

Ⓢ Calton Lees car park is strategically sited for excursions on foot in the Chatsworth area, and is hugely popular. A refreshment kiosk operates at busy times. **From the car park entrance cross the cattle-grid and descend to the Derwent's bank by a ruined mill.** Its curious architecture belies its history: it dates from 1760 and until 1952 it ground corn for animal feeds, then stood redundant for ten years before succumbing to three giant beeches that collapsed onto it during a gale. **Turn downstream to rejoin the road at One Arch Bridge.** Like the more sumptuous Chatsworth Bridge, it was designed by James Paine in 1760.

**Cross the bridge and take a kissing-gate on the right.** Note that for a direct climb to Beeley Hilltop, omitting the village, keep straight on the road to Beeley Lodge, ahead, then climb up the road alongside.

**From the kissing-gate a fieldpath heads away through a vast pasture to join the road again just short of Beeley. Cross straight over and up the narrow road past the church.**

Beeley has a keen 'estate' feel to it, indeed much of it was designed in the mid-19th century by Joseph Paxton on behalf of the 6th Duke of Devonshire. St. Anne's church was restored in 1884, but retains a Norman doorway and 14th century tower. Attractive cottages abound, and buildings of note include the early 17th century Old Hall, with mullioned and transomed windows. Village pub is the *Devonshire Arms* (surprise!), and opposite are some strikingly characterful almshouses. There is also a former Wesleyan Chapel of 1890.

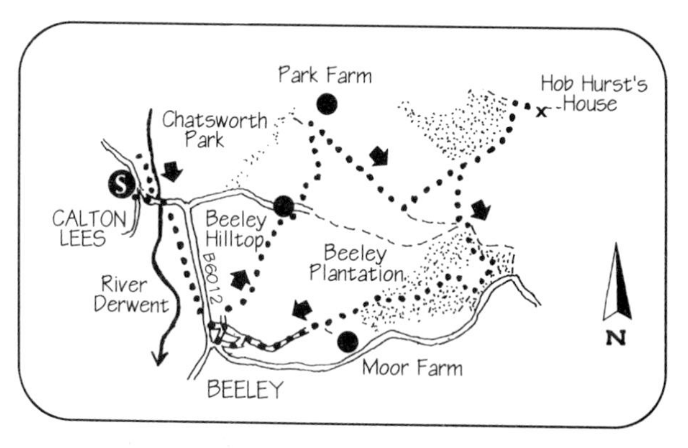


**At the top go left on the narrow road to a few houses, then quickly take a stile set back on the right. A path crosses to another such stile, then bear left to the top corner.** There are good views over the village backed by Stanton Moor. **Slant left to another corner stile, and continue up a larger field to pass by a stile in the opposite wall, continuing up to a gate at the top. Beeley Hilltop appears ahead, fronted by the imposing early 18th century house. Follow the track along to the farmyard, and keep right of the buildings. Just short of the lane a stile on the right sees us cross the edge of an enclosure to another stile onto the rough road.**

**Go right just 25 yards and take a stile on the left. From here to Beeley Brook we are on concession paths. Rise up the field to a stile to enter the dense bracken flank of the Rabbit Warren. A good path rises left to gain the distinct edge.** This is a fine place to linger, with views back over the valley. **Joining a broad track, turn right on the moor edge.** The modest outcrops overlooking Beeley Hilltop are not seen unless venturing a few yards to the edge.

**Part way along, another sign sends a thinner, waymarked path off across the moor. It runs to a junction by a simple wooden bridge, to which we shall return after a visit to Hob Hurst's House. Cross the bridge and on to a stile in the corner by the plantation edge. The path rises up the wallside outside the trees, the colourful moor on our right being a wildlife sanctuary. At the very top Open Country is entered, and just yards beyond, a broad path is joined.** Revealed ahead are superb views over the rolling heather moors towards Robin Hood, Birchen Edge and other edges beyond. The heathery tract on the brow here makes an ideal place to enjoy a picnic. **Turn right on the path for just a couple of minutes to reach Hob Hurst's House.**

*Old mill by the Derwent,
Chatsworth Park*

Hob Hurst's House is a Bronze Age burial mound surrounded by a square outer bank and ditch. These enclose a stone lined grave (cist) which when excavated in 1853 revealed human bones. Though only one of many such cairns on the moors, its easily identifiable layout in the heather makes it something of a feature on these otherwise lonely moors. Its individual name adds further intrigue, recalling a mythical elf who haunted the nearby woods.

On leaving retrace outward steps down to the path junction over the bridge, and this time go left. The path runs down, becoming sunken to join the firm track vacated earlier. Go left, joining a rough road beyond a stile. Cross straight over to a green path into the trees. At an early fork remain on the higher, broader path. This passes above a clearing giving fine views over the wooded side valley of Beeley Brook and down to the village. The path runs on to cross the brook.

Just beyond, keep right and the path soon drops down through denser trees to a junction. Go right here, descending a super path to join the beck as it eases out after a steep, deeply enclosed plunge. On fording the beck the green path runs on to a gate out of the trees. Turn left down the track, which runs down to join Moor Farm drive. Continue on this back road to enter the village. Either keep straight on this road to arrive back by the church, or to visit the pub's environs turn left down a narrow road at the first chance, then running alongside the brook again to get there.

To conclude, head up the street opposite the pub to a tiny triangular green. Bear left to return to the junction above the church, from where retrace steps to One Arch Bridge. On crossing, go straight ahead to find a path climbing the steep wooded bank to the garden centre end of the car park.

*St. Anne's, Beeley*

## 9

# STANAGE (SOUTH)

***START*** *Hathersage* *Grid ref. SK 231814*

***DISTANCE*** *6½ miles*

***ORDNANCE SURVEY MAPS***
*1:50,000*
*Landranger 110 - Sheffield & Huddersfield*
*1:25,000*
*Outdoor Leisure 1 - Peak District, Dark Peak*

***ACCESS*** *Start from the village centre. There is a car park. Served by Sheffield-Castleton buses and a number of less frequent services. Also has its own station on the Hope Valley line (Sheffield-Manchester).*
*• ACCESS AREA - see page 8.*

An outstanding walk atop a fine gritstone edge, enhanced by the lovely climb from and return to the valley.

Ⓢ Hathersage is a popular village, more for its surroundings than its own inherent appeal: it is certainly not a 'tourist' village in the style of Castleton. Hathersage is perhaps best known as the home of Little John, and the last resting place of Robin Hood's lieutenant. Set back from the main street is the neat St. Michael's Catholic church of 1806, which replaced a 1692 chapel that was destroyed by local mobs. Most attractive architecturally of several pubs is the *George Hotel*. Alongside it is a rare preserved cheese press, while the junction outside boasts a fine old roadsign and lamp standard.

**Head east along the main street (A625) as far as the *Hathersage Inn*, behind which turn along Baulk Lane. This quickly becomes a rough lane, which is left after 200 yards by a surfaced path climbing up the fieldsides to the parish church. The path enters the yard and runs along the front of the church.**

The church of St. Michael & All Angels is a fine building on a lofty eminence, a landmark in this part of the valley. Parts of the church, notably the 14th century tower, survived mid-19th century restoration. Internally it appears smaller than expected, but nevertheless a delightful place, best known for some outstanding 15th and 16th century brasses of the Eyre family. Almost opposite the door is the grave of Little John. It is said he was born and raised in the village, later returning for his final years. Note also the shaft of an ancient cross.

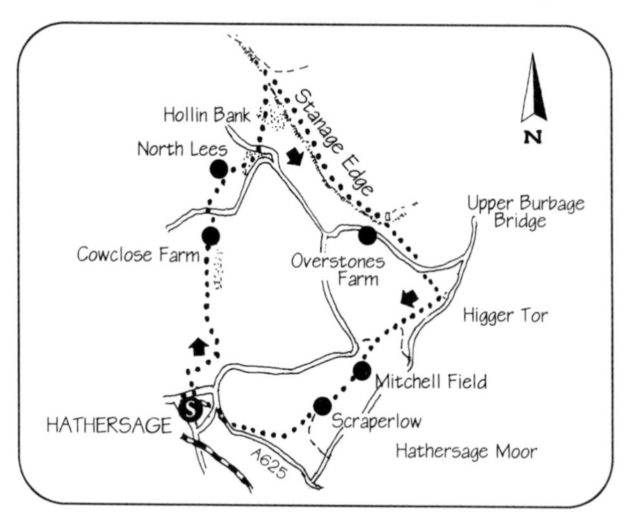


**Emerging by the church gate onto a narrow lane, go left to a bend, take a stile in front and go right a short way.** On the right is the grassy bank of Camp Green, a circular encampment of ancient origin. **Before opening out into the field branch left through a gap, down a few old steps and down the field to a slab footbridge on a tiny brook. Head away up the fieldside, the thin path bearing right across the centre to a fence-stile at the end. Rise to join an old green way which runs on to enter a large field beneath Birchin Wood. Advance along the field bottom to Cowclose Farm.**

Down to the left is the big house of Brookfield Manor: this Victorian residence incorporates parts of a 17th century house, and is now a conference centre. Up ahead, North Lees Hall is seen beneath the enticing wall of Stanage Edge. Both will soon be ours to survey.

**Keep right of all the buildings and follow the drive out to a road.** The National Park's North Lees campsite is just to the right. **Go left 50 yards then climb again on the drive to North Lees Hall.** This splendid old hall dates from 1594 and was one of several in the area owned by the influential Eyre family. It is best known for a visit by Charlotte Bronte in 1845 (while staying in Hathersage), and played a role as Thornfield Hall in her classic novel *Jane Eyre*. The restored building is now let out as holiday accommodation, and on rare occasions is open to the public.

*North Lees Hall*

**The drive climbs above the hall to a farm: don't enter but double back right up into a field. A green, part paved path slants away to the top corner to enter a wood. Rise through this to emerge onto another road, though near the top a little short-cut path climbs left to join the road at a toilet block.**

**Cross straight over the road into Open Country. With Stanage Edge now just above, rise up open ground to join a prominent worn path rising from Hollin Bank car park to enter Stanage Plantation. For the most part it climbs as a superb old paved way (a veritable 'climbers' causey') through woodland that resembles anything but a plantation as we know it.** This paved trod is known as Jacob's Ladder and is connected with the Long Causeway Roman road that crossed the moor here. The paving itself probably dates from 18th century packhorse use. **Emerging from the scattered woodland it continues slanting up beneath the crags to join the path along the crest.**

If not already done so, pause to take in the brilliant view: Mam Tor, Kinder Scout and Win Hill are major features across the valley, blighted only by the presence of the ubiquitous Hope Valley cement works. Looking down beyond Hathersage the well wooded valley stretches away. Don't forget to look back, from these airy stances, along the northern half of Stanage (see WALK 19), a wonderful sweep of Peakland's longest edge.

**Turn right along here for an uncomplicated march along the southern half of Stanage's delectable edge.** Climbers play extensively on these fine crags, their accessibility being a particular boon. This is one of the most important climbing areas in the country, with literally hundreds of named routes along this near four mile edge. **Both path and edge rises gradually to ultimately gain an Ordnance Survey column (S2156) at 1499ft/457m, virtually at the end of the edge.** This stands a mere metre lower than Stanage's high point, at High Neb.

En route, be sure to stray from the path (within reason) to savour some of the dramatic scenes below: don't frighten the climbers! One feature of particular note is Robin Hood's Cave, part way along where a shelf sits beneath the crest but above the main wall of crag. Here one can double back to discover a shallow hollow that affords crude shelter, at the end a hollowed bowl sheltering neatly under the edge.

The OS column, meanwhile, offers a new view ahead to Higger Tor, with Burbage Rocks North to its left. **Doubling back a few yards from the trig. point a path slants down to join another and heads away from the diminishing edge. Keep to the upper path to meet the open road east of Overstones Farm. Take a stile opposite and the main path heads across the grassy moor towards another road.**

**At a path crossroads just short of the stile don't join the road but turn right on a path running a straight course down the moor, steepening to join an enclosed green way. Continue down this, becoming a rougher lane which if retained will join a road for a direct finish. However, in the dip take the drive left to Mitchell Field.** The neat restoration of this farm, within a nature conservation area, was recognised by an award from the Council for the Protection of Rural England.

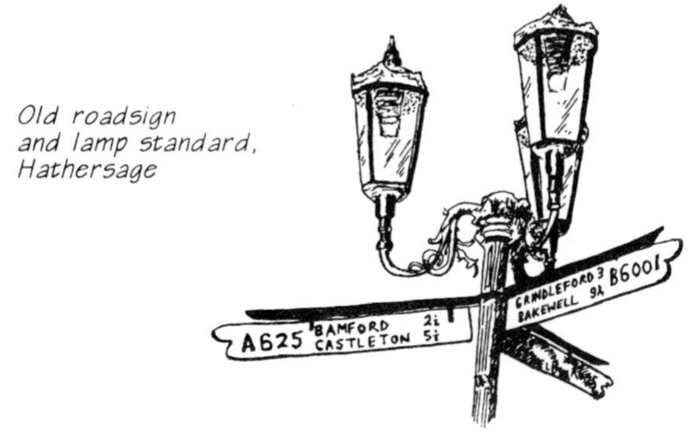


*Old roadsign and lamp standard, Hathersage*

**Stay on the drive left of the buildings, and at the rear turn right off it just short of a duckpond. A thin path runs through trees to a stile above. Cross the field to another stile then rise gently up to the brow of the rough pasture on an improving path.** There is a good view left to Owler Tor on the Hathersage Moor skyline, with the old quarry of Millstone Edge, now a climbing ground, to the right. **The path curves round beneath bracken to the architecturally intriguing and noteworthy Scraperlow Hall. Keep left around the garden wall to join its drive.**

**Head away on the drive, but when it swings left keep straight on a thin wallside path through bracken. In the very bottom corner a stile admits into woodland. The path works its way to the far bottom corner.** Deep hollowed ways come in on both sides to this point. **Continue down an old enclosed way to a house and then simply follow this access road down onto the main road on the edge of Hathersage. Go right to finish, possibly turning down Crosslands Road and then along Ibbotson's Croft at the bottom. Go right on a footway to the main road, or left for the car park.**

# 10

# A DERWENT WAY

***START*** *Grindleford* *Grid ref. SK 250788*

***FINISH*** *Bamford*

***DISTANCE*** *5¼ miles*

***ORDNANCE SURVEY MAPS***
*1:50,000*
*Landranger 110 - Sheffield & Huddersfield*
*Landranger 119 - Buxton, Matlock & Dove Dale*
*1:25,000*
*Outdoor Leisure 1 - Peak District, Dark Peak*
*Outdoor Leisure 24 - Peak District, White Peak*

***ACCESS*** *Start from Grindleford railway station and finish at Bamford railway station, both on the Hope Valley (Sheffield-Manchester) rail line. If arriving by car, Grindleford station offers better parking.*

A rare linear walk, taking advantage of railway stations and riverside footpaths to trace the beautiful Derwent up through a sylvan paradise.

**S** **Leave the station by the private road over the railway.** For the short walk to Padley Chapel, please see the identical start to WALK 1 on page 12. The chapel is also featured and illustrated in that chapter.

**Over the cattle-grid just past the chapel, take a gate on the left to cross the railway by a high stone bridge, with the signal box just down to the left. Descending the field beyond, leave the track before the trees, passing through a gateway to cross to the far corner. Go left with the wall, curving gently down and a path forming as bracken is entered. In the very corner ignore a farm bridge over a side stream and take a stile on the right to join the Derwent. Turn upstream, clinging to the riverbank through a vast pasture.**

This section is a real gem, so peaceful yet so accessible and surrounded by civilisation (road up to the left, railway up to the right). Up to the right are the massed woods of the National Trust's Longshaw estate with a glimpse of the cliffs of Lawrencefield Quarry on the skyline ahead. **At the end of the pasture we enter Coppice Wood, a delightful spell before emerging into another large pasture.**

**Soon we cut a big sweep of the river, and with a wall on the right, cross directly towards the fine looking house of Harper Lees. Pass to its left to join its drive, this leads out past abandoned masonry and re-unites with the river to join the B6001.** This midway point suggests a detour into Hathersage (right), but the nearest refreshments are just a minute away at the *Plough Inn* across Leadmill Bridge. On crossing the bridge look downstream to see Millstone Edge perfectly framed.

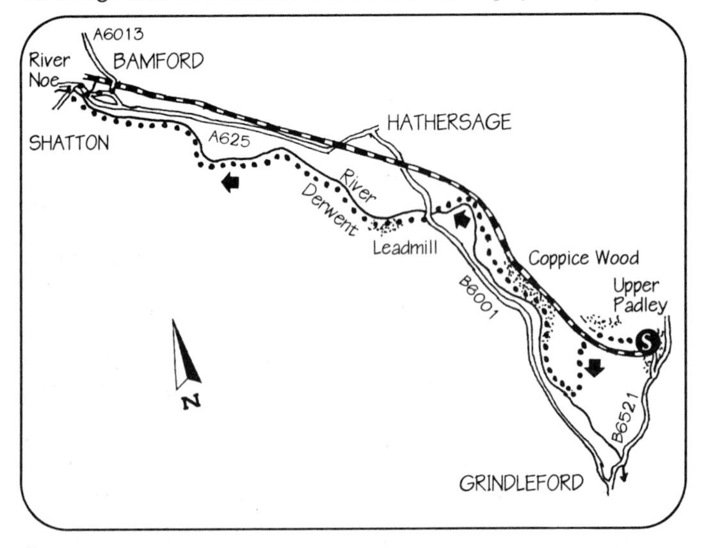


**Across Leadmill Bridge take a stile and resume up the opposite bank. This too remains hard by the river, and after an early deflection by a steep wooded bank, runs on, at times narrowly, between fields and river.** Ahead are views of both Lose Hill and Win Hill, with Grindslow Knoll on Kinder Scout jutting out directly above Back Tor. **At a guidepost we meet a crossroads, for down to the right is a fine set of almost three dozen stepping stones tempting a crossing. In more**

**open relaxed surrounds the path runs on, enjoying a grand woodland spell along the way.** Across the valley, Bamford Edge rises impressively.

*Stepping stones, River Derwent*

**Emerging after a tiny stream, loop round a vast pasture passing isolated Kentney Barn. Another stream crossing and more undulating woodland follows. At the end the path is deflected straight ahead by a tiny sidestream, then crossing it to run on to a stile onto the back road to Shatton. Turn right over the bridge to the A625.** This stream is not the Derwent but the Noe, which slipped into the main river after we parted company. **Cross to the garden centre and go right on the footway to Mytham Bridge.** Here, appropriately, we have a parting look at the Derwent. **Across the parallel footbridge turn left up a side-lined section of old road to join the A6013 up into Bamford village.**

On the open grass here stand three gateposts from the tollgate that stood by the bridge on the Sheffield-Sparrowpit-Manchester turnpike of 1758. They were recovered from their original position and placed here in 1985. **Though Bamford village centre is actually another half mile up the road, the station is found almost at once.** If your train's a long way off, the rambling *Marquis of Granby* pub sits just down to the right at the road junction. Bamford village is dominated by the tall slim spire of its church of St. John the Baptist, dating from 1861. There are two pubs in the village centre, the *Derwent Hotel* and the *Anglers Rest,* and several shops.

# 11

# DERWENT EDGE

***START*** *Strines* *Grid ref. SK 220909*

***DISTANCE*** *6¾ miles*

***ORDNANCE SURVEY MAPS***
*1:50,000*
*Landranger 110 - Sheffield & Huddersfield*
*1:25,000*
*Outdoor Leisure 1 - Peak District, Dark Peak*

***ACCESS*** *Start from a car park at Strines Bridge, a quarter-mile north of the Strines Inn. Summer Sunday/BH Monday buses from Sheffield.*
*• Some of the upland section of this walk is on the National Trust's Derwent estate, where walkers enjoy open access subject to by-laws.*

A high level, almost exclusively moorland walk, with the scent of the heather prevalent and long distance views the order of the day.

**S** **Leave the car park by the private road climbing into the trees, a dead-end bridleway! This proves a stiff start as it rises through a broad gap in the plantations. It is, however, the only steep work (indeed, almost the only work) of the walk. On easing out it runs on to a stile at a gate onto the moor.** A notice firmly points out that there is no right to roam off the path.

**The rough road climbs left to a shooting cabin, while happily our more inviting green track runs straight on over the moor. This section is entirely straightforward as we simply remain on the rising track of Foulstone Road.** All around is classic rolling heather moorland, with a glimpse of Back Tor on the skyline ahead to the right, and then the Wheel Stones over to the left. Salubrious grouse butts to the right feature wooden gates! Passed on the left is a standing stone with a small inscribed boundary stone (WF) leaning against it.

**In time the way becomes a normal walkers' path, climbing a little more steeply then running on to reach the summit of the path at Bradfield Gate Head on Derwent Edge, marked by a boundary stone.** This is the finest moment as the view west finally opens out, revealing the sombre moors of the Dark Peak including a great Kinder skyline, the Mam Tor ridge and down our impending Derwent Edge path to Dovestone Tor. **Back Tor's white trig. point became visible only yards before the summit, just minutes up to the right. Although it is visited from the Derwent Valley in WALK 14, few are likely to ignore its proximity on this walk.**

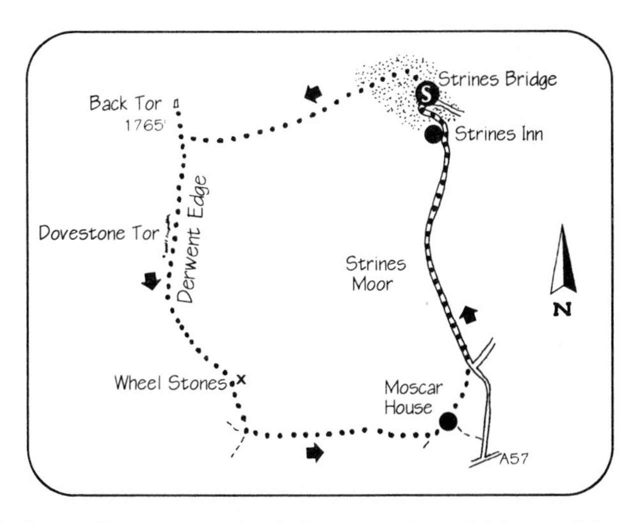


Back Tor offers a group of rocks far more substantial than anticipated. Indeed the Ordnance Survey column (S2145) at 1765ft/538m is cemented onto the topmost rock requiring a simple scramble. There are sufficient boulders piled about to permit an hour or so's scrambling of all levels. This is a classic spot, with sweeping views into Peakland and interesting ones out, notably eastwards to the tower blocks of the city of Sheffield.

**Retrace steps to the path crossroads and this time remain on the part flagged Derwent Edge path, leading past the Cakes of Bread outcrops in the heather to reach the bouldery crest of Dovestone Tor.** Enjoy a good prospect down into Dovestones Clough and beyond to

Ladybower Reservoir. **Leaving here our next objective, the Salt Cellar, appears silhouetted more clearly on the edge just minutes away. This celebrated landmark sits just beneath a collection of rocks, and is illustrated on page 68.** The path thereto is unmade, as at this point we leave National Trust land. From here to leaving the ridge beyond the Wheel Stones we are on neither right of way nor access land, but a long established path that has enjoyed common usage over many decades: please don't stray onto the open moor to the east.

*Wheel Stones, Derwent Edge*

**From the Salt Cellar the broad path resumes along the edge, passing White Tor and the Wheel Stones to reach another path crossroads in a dip.** White Tor is a fine craggy outcrop, particularly well sited for viewing Ladybower Reservoir with Ashopton Viaduct slotting in under Win Hill, and Bamford Edge beneath Stanage Edge. Just two minutes further, the Wheel Stones are quite superb, a chain of rocks resembling a coach and horses racing across the moor: indeed, many folk refer to them as the 'Coach and Horses'. The largest, nearest one is a monstrous 30ft high. Ample scrambling opportunities again!

**Just below, in the slight dip, a guidepost marks a crossroads with the Derwent-Moscar path. Here we must take leave of the edge and head back over the moor. Turning left, a fine path heads off through the heather, past shooting butts and descending ever gradually as it goes. Reaching the start of a track just after a boundary stone, remain on the footpath to descend past more shooting butts before merging into the track. Crossing a small stream it runs pleasantly on again to a gate off the moor. The track then drops down to a path crossroads at a bend, marked by an old guidepost.**

**Simply remain on the main track, bearing left to run along to Moscar House. Pass straight up the yard onto a green walled way rising away. At the top we return to heather moor, and a thinner path runs**

**on with a fence to arrive at a gate onto the Strines road.** It is joined at a T-junction with a branch to the enchantingly named Ughill and Dungworth.

**Turn left along the road to conclude the walk: both verges and traffic are in fairly short supply.** The road runs along the moorside and affords fine views eastwards over Strines Reservoir, built in 1871 with a capacity of 513 million gallons; and also over Dale Dyke Dam into Bradfield Dale and beyond (subject of WALK 16). Also clearly visible is the hilltop Boot's Folly, a tower built by Charles Boot in 1927 to keep his stonemasons busy. In the line of sight ahead is the moorland skyline atop which is our old friend Back Tor.

*Strines Inn*

**Almost from the outset the *Strines Inn*, despite being a short mile and a half distant is only just out of sight, and the generally slightly downhill journey is quickly accomplished.** Such is the pub's isolation that anyone coming this way on foot will - if it's open - find it difficult to pass. The arms over the door are those of the Worrall family, 16th century occupants of an earlier building here. **From the pub to the car park it is but a further five minutes along the road.** At the top of the deep clough beyond the pub is a small stone inscribed *'take off'*. This marks the point when brakes could be safely released in the days of horse-drawn coaches.

# 12

# UPPER BURBAGE

***START*** *Longshaw Lodge* *Grid ref. SK 266800*

***DISTANCE*** *5 miles*

***ORDNANCE SURVEY MAPS***
*1:50,000*
*Landranger 110 - Sheffield & Huddersfield*
*Landranger 119 - Buxton, Matlock & Dove Dale (only just)*
*1:25,000*
*Outdoor Leisure 1 - Peak District, Dark Peak*
*Outdoor Leisure 24 - Peak District, White Peak (only just)*

***ACCESS*** *Start from the National Trust car park at Longshaw Lodge, on the B6055 just off the A625 at Fox House Inn. Sheffield-Bakewell and Sheffield-Buxton buses pass the car park entrance, while Sheffield-Castleton buses stop at the start of the Duke's Drive, plum on route. Alternative starts with car parking are the Fox House Inn and Upper Burbage Bridge. • ACCESS AREA -* *see page 8.*

Largely on good moorland paths, this makes a grand evening walk to savour sunsets and watch climbers. It is entirely in South Yorkshire and almost entirely on public paths, regardless of access agreements.

**S A path runs from the bottom of the car park into trees and down over a stone arched bridge to a junction behind the house: the visitor centre is just round the front.** For a note on Longshaw Lodge, please refer to page 20. **From the visitor centre turn right on the surfaced drive to reach the gatehouse.** Views over to the left feature Eyam Moor rising across the Derwent Valley, while nearer to hand are the landmarks of Hathersage Moor, namely Over Owler Tor and, more relevantly, Higger Tor overtopping Carl Wark. Behind a tree opposite the gatehouse is a stone guidepost dated 1737 and inscribed Sheffield, Tideswell, Hope and Dronfield.

**Cross the B6521 and head off on a broad path through the trees. Part way on as the path drops left a little, bear right on a green, contouring path. This runs along to join the parallel A625.** Just up to the right at the top is the *Fox House Inn*. Built in 1773 by local man George Fox, it was known as the *Travellers Rest* until named after its builder some years later. It is popular with rock climbers recuperating after their exertions on Burbage's nearby rockfaces.

**Cross to a tiny parking area where a broad track, the Duke's Drive, heads away. Ignore this and turn a few yards up the road to another footpath sign, pointing to a stile into Open Country. A green track rises across the colourful moor.** This old quarrymans' track affords a fine view over the walk ahead, featuring Carl Wark, Higger Tor and Burbage North.

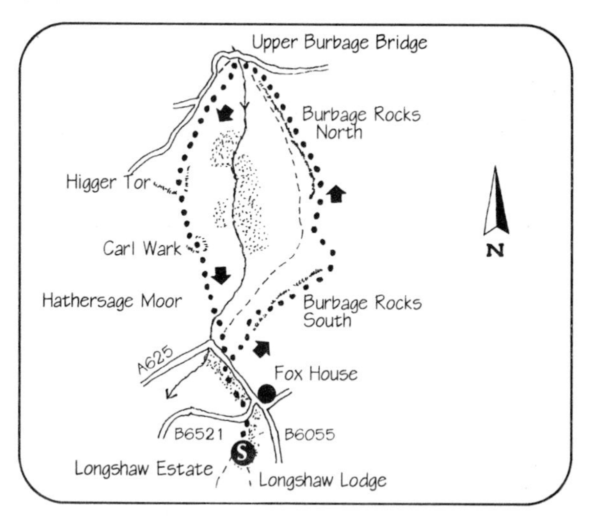


**At a junction keep left on the main track, which runs on to arrive at two neighbouring quarries beneath the edge: keep on the higher one to reach the second quarry.** The first quarry sports an improbable overhang known as the Cioch, which presents tough challenges to climbers at the very upper limits of their craft. Both quarries exhibit abandoned millstones, fashioned from the rocks into very precise circles but in the end made redundant by the arrival of fresh grinding methods.

**After the second quarry only a thinner climbers' path runs on: here is the best time to scramble up onto the edge where a good path is found. Simply head north-east along the well defined edge, passing further climbing edges.** Views west look to the Mam Tor ridge and Win Hill overtopped by the Kinder plateau, all to the left of Carl Wark.

*Stone trough on Carl Wark, looking to Higger Tor*

**Almost within yards the edge abates, and a sea of heather separates us from the northern Burbage Rocks. The path drops left with the vestiges of an old wall to a couple of large cairns on a path junction. The top one sends the public footpath up to the right to cross to the Houndkirk Road. Drop to the other cairn just below, then as the public footpath doubles back left keep straight on the thinner contouring path, our natural line (still with a vestige of a wall).**

**The path slants gently down to cross a stream, then rises again to gain the start of the northern rocks. The way runs grandly along this crest, watching again for climbers as the high point is traversed.** Look back to see the southern rocks on a long, tilted slant, and down beneath our crags to see a wealth of luxuriant foliage. The view is exclusively westwards, stretching almost the breadth of Peakland.

**Continue on as the rocks again abate to reach the road at Upper Burbage Bridge. Here the Duke's Drive also arrives. There is no need to set foot on the road itself, as a path cuts round beneath both bridges to cross the two streams on boulders. At the roadside stile at the other side take the broad path rising gently across the moor, holding the left-hand option above a stony brow before reaching a**

**knoll with Higger Tor rising across a minor saddle ahead. The path runs directly to it, climbing a restored section to gain the flat top. Keep left to reach the far end, looking down on Carl Wark.** At 1423ft/434m this is the summit of the walk, though only just.

**The direct route clambers down through the boulders to the overworn path running down to Carl Wark, though another option is to go right/west along the southern edge to a break in the rocks, and take a gentler bracken path running down to meet the main one nearer Carl Wark. A little col sits before the upthrust, which is gained alongside a section of wall.** For notes on Carl Wark please refer to page 72.

**Cross eastward along the plateau-like top to the craggy edge, then descend with care to see the direct path running down towards our entry point onto the moor. It crosses Burbage Brook in novel fashion then rises to join the Duke's Drive. Go right back to the lay-by and the road and retrace steps back to Longshaw Lodge.**

*The Leaning Buttress, Higger Tor*

13

# HASSOP & PILSLEY

***START*** *Calver* *Grid ref. SK 247744*

***DISTANCE*** *6½ miles*

***ORDNANCE SURVEY MAPS***
*1:50,000*
*Landranger 119 - Buxton, Matlock & Dove Dale*
*1:25,000*
*Outdoor Leisure 24 - Peak District, White Peak*

***ACCESS*** *Start from the old bridge on the Derwent linking Calver and Curbar. Reasonable parking on the old road, immediately upstream of the modern bridge on the A623. Served by bus from Sheffield, Chesterfield, Buxton, Bakewell and other less frequent services.*

Sub-titled *The Bluebell Way*, this walk through a springtime paradise on delightful pathways is a gem in any season.

S Calver Bridge spans the Derwent at the eastern end of the village, its 18th century arches happily by-passed by the busy road. On the east bank are the village school, church and pub, the aptly named *Bridge Inn*. All Saints church dates from 1868 and is shared between Calver, Curbar and Froggatt. On the west bank are shops, a cafe and a craft centre, while just behind stands Calver Mill. This enormous cotton mill was built by Richard Arkwright in 1804 after fire destroyed the 1785 mill. It was used for filming the TV series *Colditz* in the 1970s.

Calver is an outspread village, more of which will be seen as the walk progresses. Off our route, Calver also boasts the *Derwentwater Arms* and the *Eyre Arms*, the latter, along with several eating establishments and an outdoor shop, found in the higher part of the village towards Calver Sough.

**From the bridge a riverbank path leads downstream under the modern road bridge, then immediately climb steps to the roadside. Head along the road into Calver, turning left at the side road into Calver village. This runs pleasantly on as Main Street to reach the centre of the old village.** En route we pass numerous desirable residences and cottage gardens; Calver Methodist Church, erected as a Jubilee Primitive Methodist Chapel in 1860; and a house that was once the *Bulls Head.*

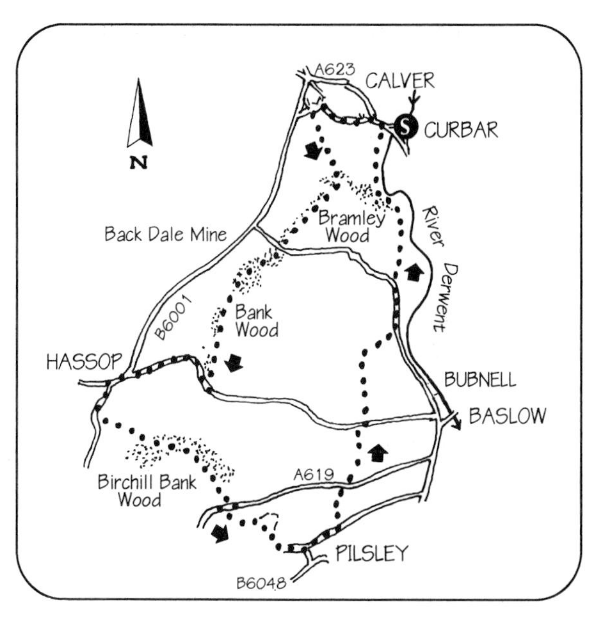


The village centre is marked by a 1977 Jubilee lamp on a sturdy gritstone buttercross type base outside the little Post office: a Victorian postbox still functions on the wall. **Swing left on High Street, up past Lowside and 50 yards beyond (just short of Cross Lane), turn left on a drive to the houses at Folds Farm. At the end a path slips round to the left of the buildings and on to a stile into a field. A path heads away with the wall, continuing on past it and down to a dip.** Over to the left Curbar and Baslow Edges are well spread. **Up the other side the path climbs to the bottom corner of a wood then rises to meet a broader path.**

The first surround of bluebells makes a dazzling display in spring. **Go left up the broad path, swinging round at the top to emerge on an open nab.** Northwards is a fine prospect over Calver to Eyam Edge and along the eastern edges. Froggatt and Curbar Edges lurk just to the right. Draped in bluebells, it was worth the whole walk for this moment alone, though it is in fact only the beginning.

**The delectable path heads away along the wallside, commencing a half-mile ramble along a defined ridge atop Bramley Wood. With a wall on the left and views over to Chatsworth and its woods and higher moors, the path runs on into woodland.** Throughout the ensuing ridge the unbroken bluebell display is a joy; the mix of bluebell and rhododendron for a while is rather bizarre. **Simply amble on to arrive at a minor road (Bramley Lane) at a nick.**

*Dower House, Hassop*

**Across the other side head away on a broader woodland track. Within a couple of minutes a stile sees us across to our original side of the wall to resume as before, this time tramping on through Bank Wood. The sounds of a quarry across the valley are happily not joined by the sight, which is masked until emerging onto an open bank. In and out of woodland the path runs on, ever gently declining to eventually reach a hurdle-stile out of the trees. Just ahead a stile admits onto School Lane.**

**Go right, descending beneath the wood to drop down to meet the B6001 on the edge of Hassop. The *Eyre Arms* offers a welcome straight ahead.** Hassop Hall dates largely from the early 19th century but parts remain from two centuries earlier. Once the home of the influential Eyre family, it is currently an up-market hotel/restaurant. The former private chapel on the roadside is now the Roman Catholic All Saints church, built in classical style for the Eyres in 1816-18. Hassop had its own station, a mile from the village on the Midland Railway's London-Manchester line via Buxton. It was built in 1863, principally to serve Chatsworth House. Plans to run the line through the grounds of Chatsworth fell foul of the Duke of Devonshire, and thus this was the nearest they got. The line closed in 1968, but now serves feet, wheels and hooves as the Monsal Trail (see *Central Peak*).

**Advance along the footway, past church and hall entrance and down to the left as far as Home Farm.** On the right is the attractive Dower House, which belonged to Hassop Hall. **Immediately after the farm take a rough lane on the left. Beyond a couple of gates it runs along a fieldside before becoming an enclosed byway down to a tiny brook, with ford and slab footbridge. Up the other side a broad forest track heads away through Birchill Bank Wood.** These increasingly grand woodlands offer more bluebells in fine form again.

**Emerging, the track runs on to meet the busy A619 Bakewell-Baslow road. Go right for a hundred yards and cross to a secretive rough lane (Bradley Lane) heading away. Crossing tiny Rymas Brook it rises gently away, climbing a big dog-leg to reach the brow just beyond which is Pilsley. Part way along the bottom of the old way a stile on the right, if located, sends a short-cut footpath up the fields to a stile by a gate at the top.**

**Pilsley is entered in some surprise, appearing straight in front at the last moment. Descend from the lanehead to the junction.** On the left is the *Devonshire Arms*, confirmation that this is very much an estate village of Chatsworth (largely an 18th century creation of the 4th Duke of Devonshire), right down to the paintwork. Along to the right are a quaint Post office/shop and a green suitable for reposing after a pint. The Chatsworth estate also has a farm shop here.

**From the pub junction bear left on the road descending out of the village. Beyond the last house note the old well, and continue down just as far as a barn on the right. Here take a stile on the left and head**

**along the wall-side to a couple of stiles just short of the end. A thin path slants down the pasture to find a stile and tiny footbridge on Rymas Brook back onto the A619.**

*The Devonshire Arms, Pilsley*

**Cross to the same pairing opposite and slant up the steep field to find a corner stile. Go on with the right-hand wall, twisting and then running on to a narrow corner stile onto a back road. Go right briefly then take a gap-stile on the left. Cross to a wall-corner, then on to a stile and along a longer field bottom.** Throughout this section we have fine views over to the right to Baslow and Curbar Edges. **From the end slant down to a stile below, then bear left down the field to the far corner behind the farm at Bubnell. The little lane heads away onto a farm road, going right to meet the through road.**

**Turn left out of tiny Bubnell, on a narrow and quite rough little road. The wood on the left gives us more bluebells, before reaching a corner. Here take a stile on the right and a path crosses the field to meet a broader way beyond another stile. This continues on, soon beneath a wooded bank where our favourite flowers give one grand finale. The river Derwent is met at a sharp bend and followed upstream to return to the start.**

14

# DERWENT EDGE

***START*** *Ladybower Reservoir* *Grid ref. SK 172892*

***DISTANCE*** *9¾ miles*

***ORDNANCE SURVEY MAPS***
*1:50,000*
*Landranger 110 - Sheffield & Huddersfield*
*1:25,000*
*Outdoor Leisure 1 - Peak District, Dark Peak*

***ACCESS*** *Start from the Fairholmes visitor centre car park at the head of Ladybower Reservoir in the Upper Derwent Valley. This is the main car park for the upper dale, 2 miles off the A57. Served by infrequent Sheffield-Castleton buses and by numerous seasonal services, the most regular being from Sheffield. Most of the upland section of this walk is on the National Trust's Derwent estate, where walkers enjoy open access subject to by-laws.*

Derwent Edge presents the finest escarpment in the upper reaches of the Derwent, and its heathery traverse is a classic high above the string of reservoirs.

**S** Fairholmes is the main focal point for visitors to the upper Derwent Valley. Here there is a small visitor centre (jointly run by Severn-Trent Water and the National Park), refreshment kiosk, toilets, cycle hire and ranger base. Ladybower Reservoir was the Upper Derwent's third and final sheet of water, completed in 1945.

**From the bottom end of the buildings a footpath runs along through trees to meet the Derwent access road. Turn right on it, over the bridge to be faced by the mighty stone Derwent Dam. Cross to the right corner where steps lead up onto a path. Go left to rise onto the rough road at the foot of the reservoir.** This bridleway runs the full length of both Derwent and Howden reservoirs to Slippery Stones, a very popular bikers' route: you are likely to see many families and novices attempting embryonic bike runs.

**Turn left on it and enjoy a prolonged saunter almost the length of Derwent Reservoir.** We have fine views over the reservoir, completed in 1916 four years after Howden Reservoir immediately above it. The slopes on the right are extensively planted, with little opportunity to savour the heather slopes just above: don't worry, we'll soon make up for that! Opposite is an inlet formed by Ouzelden Clough: note the supports, at low water levels, of a railway that served the construction of the Derwent and Howden dams. here too, now gone without trace, stood the temporary Birchinlee village, built to house reservoir construction workers and their families.

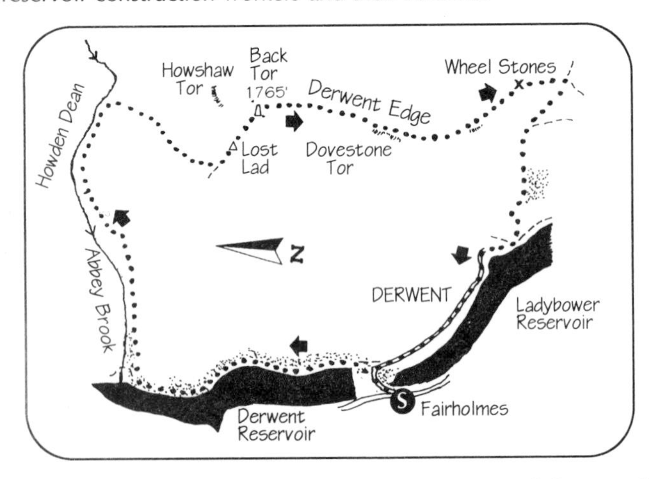


**Shortly after the near-identical castellated towers of the Howden dam appear ahead, the track loses sight of the reservoir just short of Abbey Brook Bridge. Before it drops down we take our leave, turning up a signposted footpath on the right. Two paths actually depart here: ours remains on the pleasant green track angling away, soon bearing right to rise up through trees and quickly emerge via a gateway onto the open moor.** What a contrast - steep heather slopes and an absence of human beings. No matter how many folk were milling about Fairholmes and even the reservoir track, we probably lost them all the minute we stepped off the reservoir track.

**At once the ways fork: take the more inviting grassy track running left above the plantation wall. This runs on into Howden Dean, a major side valley featuring Abbey Brook.** This is so named as Abbey Farm, a grange of Nottinghamshire's Welbeck Abbey, once stood at the valley foot. Our splendid track was built to convey shooting parties with their ponies up to the high moors. **As the path runs past the trees it can be seen scaling the slopes ahead, every step an inviting one drawing us deeper into the hills.** Note the contrast also in valley flanks: opposite is woodland and bracken, while our higher slopes offer a carpet of heather. **Remain on the path which climbs away before being forced to lose height to negotiate Cogman Clough.**

**The path resumes on a level contour, and rounding a bend opposite the attractive if curiously named Gravy Clough, the upper reaches of the dale appear with Berristors Tor prominent in the narrowing section.** Now, more than before, we realise the scale of Howden Dean. **Opposite the modest rock outcrop the path is forced up to the right by an intriguing landslip. At the back of it the path forks just short of the stream.** This makes a fine place to take stock. The left branch crosses the stream and resumes up the clough, its course obvious as it scales steeper flanks ahead. **At this point we finally leave the clough and opt for the right branch, which rises through bracken into the side valley of Sheepfold Clough.**

**Directly ahead is the prominent cliff of Howshaw Tor, an impressive objective. However, our way climbs thinly to the right, easing out and becoming much clearer as it curves round up onto the brow.** Views now open out to the right/west, featuring the vast heights of the Bleaklow massif across the Derwent Valley. Note also the head of Howden Dean now 180 degrees behind us! **With the white trig. on Back Tor visible over to the left on the skyline beyond Howshaw Tor, the splendid path rises onto Lost Lad Hillend, where it meets a flagged path for the final tiny pull onto Lost Lad.**

Illustrated on page 3, this grand knoll (1699ft/518m) is marked by a cairn and a memorial topograph, with Back Tor now just minutes away on the main edge. The name recalls the legend of a young Derwent boy who perished on the moors after bravely setting out from his snowbound community to tend sheep. A shepherd found his remains by a rock crudely scratched 'Lost Lad', and began a tradition of depositing a stone here, hence the cairn. Savour the view before leaving, for this is a fine detached vantage point: Derwent Edge runs from Howshaw Tor past Back Tor to our impending route past Dovestone Tor. Across the Derwent are Win Hill, the individual tops of the Mam Tor ridge, and of course Kinder's eastern end.

**The built path runs through a dip then up onto the edge to find Back Tor set well back, and the Ordnance Survey column surmounting a grouping of rocks far more substantial than anticipated.** Indeed the trig. (S2145) at 1765ft/538m is cemented onto the topmost rock and requires a simple scramble to attain. There are sufficient boulders piled about to permit an hour or so's scrambling of all levels. This is a classic spot, with sweeping views into Peakland and interesting ones out, notably east to the tower blocks of the city of Sheffield.

*The Salt Cellar, Derwent Edge*

**Resume by heading south on the flagged path, leading past the Cakes of Bread outcrops in the heather to the bouldery crest of Dovestone Tor.** Enjoy a good prospect down into Dovestones Clough and beyond to Ladybower Reservoir. **Leaving here our next objective, the Salt Cellar, appears silhouetted more clearly on the edge just minutes away. This celebrated landmark sits just beneath a collection of scattered rocks.** The path thereto is unmade, as at this point we leave National Trust land. From here to leaving the ridge beyond the Wheel Stones we are on neither right of way nor access land, but an established path that has enjoyed common usage for many decades.

**From the Salt Cellar the broad path resumes along the edge, passing White Tor and the Wheel Stones to reach another path crossroads in a dip.** White Tor is a fine craggy outcrop, particularly well sited for viewing Ladybower Reservoir, with Ashopton Viaduct slotting in under Win Hill, and Bamford Edge beneath Stanage Edge. Just two minutes further, the Wheel Stones are quite superb, featuring a chain of rocks resembling a coach and horses racing across the moor. The largest, nearest one is a monstrous 30ft high. Ample scrambling opportunities again!

**Just below, in the slight dip, a crossroads with the Derwent-Moscar path is reached, marked by a guidepost. Here we must take leave of the edge and double back down to the right, as this well worn path slants down to meet a wall-side bridleway. Go right a few yards on it to a gate where it leaves the open moor.**

**Turn down through the gate and across the rough pasture on the broad path. It slants down to the far corner and then down above a plantation to approach a cluster of barns across Grindle Clough.** By now Ladybower Reservoir is outspread below. While passing through the bridle-gate, note the 1647 initialled datestone incorporated above the door on the barn. **The path runs down a field to emerge onto the rough road alongside Ladybower Reservoir.**

**Turn right along here to finish.** This is the old road of Derwent Lane, now for local access only. We pass through Millbrook, where part of the small farming village of Derwent stood before being abandoned to the murky waters: just a handful of buildings survive above water level. This was a tight-knit community of which the principal feature was Derwent Hall. Dating from 1672, it was a shooting lodge of the Duke of Norfolk, and ended its days as a youth hostel (1927-43). Much of the remains of the demolished village can still be discerned at times of low water, and leaflets offering further and fascinating information can be obtained at the Fairholmes visitor centre.

**The way becomes surfaced to run through the hamlet of Derwent.** Flowery verges and hints of days past add to the tinges of sadness at the death of a busy little community. En route we pass the Catholic church, once a school and now the village hall: note the Madonna and child in a niche above the door, and the bell still within its bellcote; several other rather select dwellings include the very attractive Old House Farm. **The Derwent Dam appears ahead to signal a return to the bridge and thus the start.**

15

# HATHERSAGE MOOR

***START*** *Surprise View, Hathersage* *Grid ref. SK 252801*

***DISTANCE*** *4 miles*

***ORDNANCE SURVEY MAPS***
*1:50,000*
*Landranger 110 - Sheffield & Huddersfield*
*Landranger 119 - Buxton, Matlock & Dove Dale*
*1:25,000*
*Outdoor Leisure 1 - Peak District, Dark Peak*
*Outdoor Leisure 24 - Peak District, White Peak*

***ACCESS*** *Start from the National Park's Surprise View car park on the A625 two miles south of Hathersage. There's a good chance of a refreshment van at popular times. Served by Sheffield-Castleton buses (bus stop at car park entrance). • ACCESS AREA - see page 8.*

Easy walking through a rich variety of scenery within such a small compass. Good paths virtually all the way.

**S From the car park entrance cross the road to enter the National Trust's Lawrence Field.** Currently under the Countryside Stewardship scheme, we are free to roam at will in this rough moorland pasture. At once a detour path runs left the few yards to explore the modest outcrops of Owler Tor.

**Commence the walk by taking the path right, paralleling the road to meet a public footpath at right-angles at the far end.** The stile in front, though not en route, gives access to the alarmingly steep edge of Lawrencefield Quarry, with a pool beneath it and surrounded by woodland. Its tall walls are a popular climbing ground offering over a hundred routes. A few old millstones lie about here: many were simply abandoned on site when newer grinding methods arrived.

**Our way, however, takes the grassy path down the side of the moor. As wall replaces fence we head into some trees. At the bottom corner ignore the gate and turn left on a thin, clear path through scattered natural woodland, soon reaching a path coming down to a gate.** Pass through to enter the woods of the Padley Gorge. Please keep to the path to avoid disturbing the National Trust's natural regeneration programme for this scarce surviving native oak woodland.

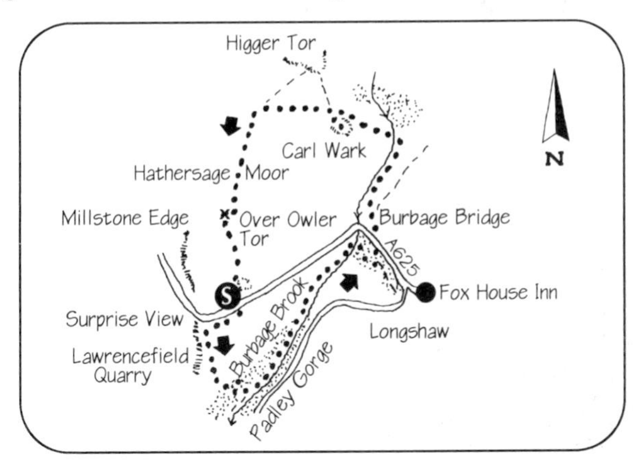


**A well made green path slants down the wood, quickly doubling back left and running down to join a busier path above Burbage Brook. Turn left on this, imperceptibly rising above the brook to suddenly emerge out of the wood. Ahead, Carl Wark and Higger Tor appear in tandem rising above the heather moorland. Passing an early footbridge, simply forge on upstream as it rises across the grassy moor.**

**Towards the top another footbridge is met, this time cross and head off up the stone path, zigzagging above the brook and into the trees. Ignore a left branch back to the nearby road, and rise gently through woodland. On easing out look for a greener path coming in from the left. Double back along this through the trees to emerge onto the A625.**

**Cross straight over to a gate to enter Open Country and head away on the broad track known as Duke's Drive. Ahead is Carl Wark, overtopped by Higger Tor. At a pair of old gateposts the direct path**

**to Carl Wark branches left for the brook. Our route takes a second path just a couple of yards further. Instead of crossing the brook it opts to trace it upstream.** The grand surrounds feature Carl Wark frowning above us, and Burbage Rocks over to the right. **The path soon reaches the foot of a plantation and drops to find a stone arched bridge on the brook.** This is a superb example of a packhorse bridge, hidden off the beaten track but clearly at one time very much on it. Note the absence of side walls to ensure unimpeded progress of laden ponies.

*Packhorse bridge, Burbage Brook*

**Cross and take the path climbing towards Carl Wark. It bears right of the craggy edge to reach a saddle just beneath the top. Double back left to gain its crest alongside a reconstructed section of wall.** Carl Wark appears a classic example of an Iron Age hillfort dating back perhaps 2500 years, but experts suggest a 5th or 6th century relic of the Dark Ages, in other words a thousand years younger!

Both claims may be right, in that an older fort was later re-established after the Romans departed, by British tribes as defence against the Anglian invaders. This natural site is defended on three sides by steep scarps of gritstone boulders, with a wide turf rampart supporting the mighty wall at the open western end, where we entered the site.

**Return to the path junction in the saddle, and just a couple of yards along the Higger Tor path, a thinner path bears left through the bracken.** Anyone not having visited Higger Tor before might consider a detour thereto, the obvious path tempting a short, direct climb onto its prow. An alternative path bears left up through bracken to the left of the southernmost boulders, with the prominent leaning buttress (illustrated on page 59) further along to the left. From the top a path leaves in similar fashion, slanting south-west through the bracken aiming for the large, walled enclosure on the moor.

**The direct path, meanwhile, broadens then narrows but runs clearly on to a junction with the path coming down off Higger Tor. Go left on this, crossing to the left side of a walled enclosure. It runs up its side, and on the minor brow above merges into another path. Go left on this along the crest of a minor ridge, running on through the heathery defile of Winyards Nick to the waiting boss of rock that is Over Owler Tor.**

*Mother Cap, Hathersage Moor*

Its easily accessible top makes a fine vantage point with the end of the walk only ten minutes away. Just to the west is the crest of the tall cliffs of Millstone Edge quarry, another workshop turned playground. This location reaches up to 100ft and boasts getting on for 200 different routes. **Resume on the path to the isolated tor of Mother Cap, from where the car park re-appears below. Descend into the trees, keeping left of a quarry with its few abandoned millstones to runs down to re-enter the car park.**

16

# BRADFIELD DALE

***START*** *Bradfield*  *Grid ref. SK 263919*

***DISTANCE*** *6 miles*

***ORDNANCE SURVEY MAPS***
*1:50,000*
*Landranger 110 - Sheffield & Huddersfield*
*1:25,000*
*Outdoor Leisure 1 - Peak District, Dark Peak*

***ACCESS*** *Start from the car park in Low Bradfield, reached along a back road - The Sands - west of the bridge in the village. Served by bus from Sheffield via Hillsborough.*

An absorbing ramble round an unsung corner of the Peak: though within the National Park the South Yorkshire feeling is strong. A reasonable amount of up and down work is involved, but glorious views are the reward. Note that several of this walk's public footpaths are omitted from the Landranger map (1993 edition).

**S From the car park return along the lane, then left down Fair House Lane to the road junction and Smithy Bridge in the village.** Low Bradfield is an attractive village owing much to the stream flowing through: this is a lovely corner where ducks dabble and children play. **Keep straight on Mill Lee Road rising past an old chapel to a junction by the *Plough Inn*. Just yards above it take an enclosed bridlepath along to the right.**

There are good views to the right of High Bradfield up the hill: we shall conclude through this settlement. **Past a cottage the track runs to a stile. As a green track rises away, a footpath keeps straight on above the beck, Dale Dike, running very pleasantly through mixed country to join a road near Annet Bridge, with its odd single sloped arch.**

**Turn left up the road (Blindside Lane) for a good three-quarter mile's walk, and after a plantation starts on the right, turn into it at the first opportunity. A slanting path, Roger Lane, drops down into the trees. When it turns left take a signed branch down to the right. Squeezing through undergrowth it immediately becomes a broad way.** Running between old walls it is a roadway lost when the reservoir was built. **At the bottom it leaves us on the shore of Dale Dyke Reservoir.** These colourful surroundings would do fair justice to a picnic.

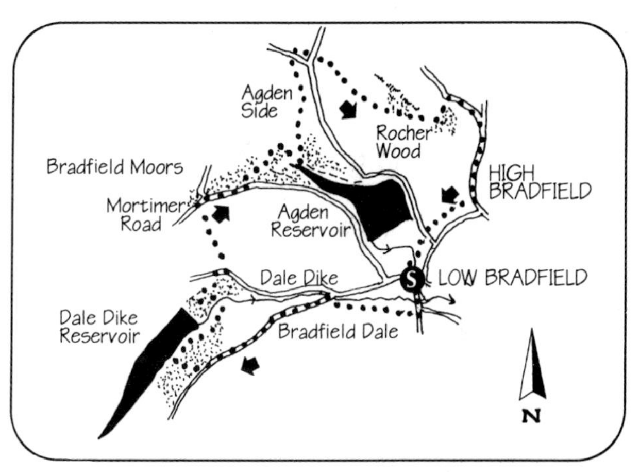


Dale Dyke Reservoir was the scene, in 1864, of the country's worst dam burst. Nearing completion, the earth embankment collapsed releasing millions of gallons downstream. Around 240 perished as the mighty tide - known as the Sheffield Flood - surged down the valleys to the city. Rebuilt in 1875, the reservoir was not brought into use for a dozen more years, and even then its capacity was less than half that of the original.

**Turn right on the path, entering deeper woodland beyond the end of the dam. The path drops down several stairs to a water outfall and runs downstream as a vehicle track to a wooden bridge. This zigzags up the opposite slope, merging with another such track to run above the trees out onto Dale Road. Go right briefly then take a gate on the left. A bridleway climbs an initially steep tract of open country.** Halt to savour views back over the reservoir to the hilltop Boot's Folly, a tower built by Charles Boot in 1927 to keep his stonemasons busy.

**Easing out at the top, a briefly enclosed way rises onto Mortimer Road, the moorside Strines road.** Look back over the gate to regain breath, and over to the left is the craggy crest above Rocher Wood: we shall be walking beneath that before the walk ends.

**Go right a few yards and then down the side road of Windy Bank. Just past Wilkin Hill (an outdoor centre) take a stile on the left. A splendid path heads off into the trees, crossing a tiny stream and then working round to a junction with a broader track. Up ahead, the moorland of Agden Side beckons us on. Cross straight over and the good path continues down to cross a surprisingly high arched bridge on Agden Dike.** Across it is the Agden Bog Nature Reserve of the Yorkshire Wildlife Trust.

**Turn downstream to reach a gate by the head of Agden Reservoir. Pass through but then leave the broad path and turn up a thinner wallside one.** Keep straight on for a quicker, easy return which would, however, sacrifice the finest moments of the walk. **The path climbs through bracken along the side of the wood, then steeply above a bend to a stile onto the open moor of Agden Side. The climbing continues a little further, and at the top the path runs left along the brow of the vast sweep of moor.** This is a stunningly lovely section, notably in late summer when the heather dominates. The valley of Agden Dike leads the eye up to Bradfield and Broomhead Moors above the Strines road. **Running atop a few minor outcrops the path ends at a stile, with a narrow back road (Agden Side Road) just above.**

**Cross straight over to another stile then bear right across the pasture to a stile onto another road. Straight across, an enclosed track (the old drive) runs to Rocher Head Farm. Pass along the front of the sad ruins, and at the end head away with a line of hawthorn trees on the right.** Agden Reservoir is prominent below, with the Rocher Wood rocks in view ahead. **Maintain this course and in the second field the faint path splits. One branch takes a stile on the right, while ours runs on to a stile ahead (quaintly still signed 'privilege footpath'). Entering dense bracken the green path runs right a little before rising away (flight of steps) to join a broader green way, with the rocks just above. All around are some fine oak trees.**

**Levelling out the path merges into another track.** From here look back south over the moors to the back of Derwent Edge with some of its rock outcrops discernible. **The track then runs away around the**

**head of Rocher End Brook's wooded clough to debouch onto a road. Go right, keeping right at a fork and descending as Brown House Lane into High Bradfield.** On the right before the first houses is the wooded knoll of Bailey Hill behind the farm. This is the site of a small motte and bailey castle built at the time of William the Conqueror.

*The Watch House, High Bradfield*

**At the head of the village turn right down cobbled Jane Street to the parish church.** High Bradfield is a charming spot feeding off its proud heritage. Some fine buildings are clustered around little cobbled streets, including the old post office and the Watch House at the church gate: it dates from 1745 and the 'watch' was for bodysnatchers! Just along Church Street is the village pub, the *Old Horns Inn*, with the village stocks facing it. The church of St Nicholas is a gem, with fine medieval beams in the Nave roof. The tower dates back around 500 years, and other features include a Norman font and a Saxon cross. With an area of 37 square miles (23,680 acres) this is claimed as the largest parish in England! It also boasts 100 miles of footpaths.

**Down past the church gate a footway runs outside the churchyard. Emerging into a field, drop just a short way to a wall corner, then squeeze through a stile by the gate and descend the wallside. From a stile at the bottom resume down the other wallside to a clearer spell above trees. Emerging, bear right with an old wall, dropping down to a pair of stiles to join a road. Cross straight over and down a snicket to emerge above the stream: steps drop down to the right to a foot-bridge. To return to the car park cross and turn downstream, for the village turn left without crossing and then go right along the road.**

17

# CHATSWORTH PARK

***START*** *Calton Lees* *Grid ref. SK 258685*

***DISTANCE*** *6¾ miles*

***ORDNANCE SURVEY MAPS***
*1:50,000*
*Landranger 119 - Buxton, Matlock & Dove Dale*
*1:25,000*
*Outdoor Leisure 24 - Peak District, White Peak*

***ACCESS*** *Start from the Calton Lees car park on the B6012 south of Baslow. Served by Calver-Matlock buses, and from Chesterfield, Bakewell and Sheffield on Summer Sundays/BH Mondays.*

A parkland ramble based on the estate village of Edensor, featuring superb views over Chatsworth and its park and a delectable riverside.

**S** **From the car park entrance cross the cattle-grid on the road and descend to the Derwent's bank by a ruined mill.** Its curious architecture belies its history: it dates from 1760 and until 1952 it ground corn for animal feeds, then stood redundant for ten years before succumbing to three giant beeches that collapsed onto it during a gale. **Turn upstream to amble through glorious surrounds, with Chatsworth House itself, seat of the Duke of Devonshire, arrayed ahead. Sumptuous! The walking soon brings us to Chatsworth Bridge.** This elegant structure was designed by James Paine in 1761. The old village of Edensor stood near here before being demolished as it interfered with the view from the house.

If this is a first visit then it is worth crossing to look at Queen Mary's Bower, one of those curiosities that adorn the English countryside. It is so named as the captive Mary, Queen of Scots found relaxation in her small garden here during spells at Chatsworth in the 1570s. Along with the Hunting Tower on the skyline, it is all that remains of Bess of Hardwick's original works at Chatsworth. It was restored about 1830 and is thought to include an ancient earthwork guarding a ford on the Derwent. For more on Chatsworth, please refer to WALK 5. **Our route turns left at the bridge, not on the drive but on a footpath that rises over the brow to approach the village of Edensor.** Down on the left, just before the road, is the only surviving house from the old village. **The path crosses to and over the B6012 to enter the village by private-looking gates and a cattle-grid at a gatehouse.**

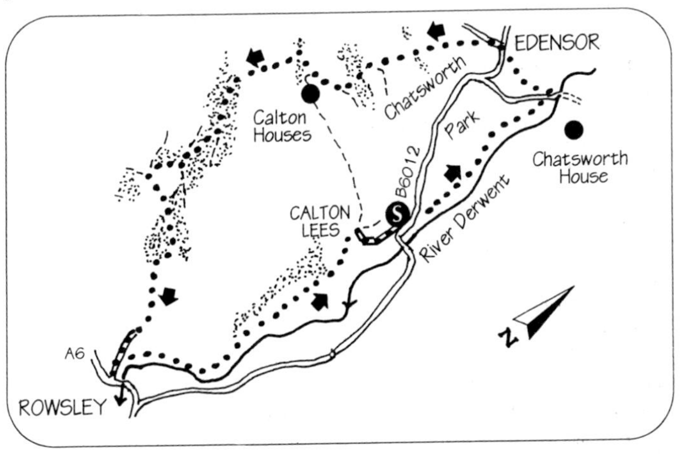


Edensor - pronounced 'En-sor' - is an estate village rebuilt by Thomas Paxton between 1838 and 1842 on behalf of the 6th Duke, an intriguing mix of architectural styles. The absorbing little place has a Post office/shop-cum-cafe tucked round a quiet corner. It also earns a little nostalgia for the author as his childhood years were spent in a humble cobbled street named Edensor Road, in a Yorkshire milltown where the Cavendish family owned land.

Dominating the village is the remarkably tall spire of St. Peter's church. It was built in 1867, the work of renowned architect Giles Gilbert Scott. Some panels inside tell, in a charming manner, much of the village's origins and layout. Seek out the Devonshire Chapel, and discover the story behind a most unlikely marble figure! A cross base by the main church path is of 13th century origin, likely to have been a preaching cross when no church stood here.

At the top of the churchyard is the Cavendish family plot, a largely unpretentious collection of various Dukes and family members. These include Frederick Cavendish, murdered in Phoenix Park, Dublin in 1882 within hours of landing (an elaborate memorial fountain stands by the roadside at Bolton Abbey, the Cavendish's famous Yorkshire estate); and Kathleen, widow of the Marquess of Hartington (the Duke's son), and sister of assasinated American president John Fitzgerald Kennedy. A plaque records his visit to his sister's grave in 1963, just prior to his own untimely end.

**Head up the main street and look for a signposted footpath *(Rowsley)* on the left. This climbs steep steps to emerge into the open park.** Fallow deer may well be seen in this open sweep. **Simply head straight up, keeping right of a long, thin plantation (occasional marker posts) to join a faint green bridleway near the top.** Before entering the trees pause to appraise the wonderful scene. The tip of Edensor's spire leads the eye up the Derwent Valley to Baslow Edge and beyond, but the main focus is undoubtedly on Chatsworth House in its inimitable setting.

**A stile into the plantation sees us rise a little more on a rough lane to emerge on a brow.** Ahead an immediate broad vista opens, looking down Calton's deep side valley. **Advance along the green track, passing a path junction and curving down to the right with a wall. Just beneath is Calton Houses, and at the bottom a gate is reached.** Here those seeking a quick finish can turn down the drive from the buildings and be back at Calton Lees within the half-hour.

*Queen Mary's Bower*

**Those of sterner stuff will ignore the gate and instead take the green track rising gently right outside the small plantation. This quickly reaches a gap between Calton Plantations. Cross the stile to the other side of the head of this valley, and a track heads away left. This soon narrows but climbs unfailingly up the bank to approach another ridgetop plantation. The path runs on to a stile into the trees of New Piece Wood.** Again, pause to look back over a wide landscape.

**A broad path heads away, quickly swinging left to run through a clearing as a grand green way. After a section in a break shared with overhead wires, the way veers right to reach a gateway on the steep edge.** With the planting of new trees here the open views south over the last couple of miles of the Wye to Stanton Moor should remain safe for a number of years. Beneath the moor with its mast, Stanton in Peak village is easily discerned, the church spire and large hall confirming its location.

**The track runs left along the wallside then drops steeply into the trees. At a junction (Haddon estate sign) go left, soon bearing right at a fork and dropping steeply again. This runs down to a crossroads of bridleways in front of a clearing (grid ref. 244669). Go left on a track between hedgerow and wall, initially on a very minor rise. At the end keep straight on into the trees at Bouns Corner, running a level course before turning down the far side of the wood. This same enclosed way drops pleasantly down towards Rowsley, enjoying open views over the fields. At the head of the village it becomes surfaced to drop down past the church to the main road.**

Rowsley is a village of two halves, once known as Great and Little Rowsley. It is split by the river Derwent, the 15th century bridge having been much widened in the 1920s. Most interest is in the older, western half (Great Rowsley), including St. Katherine's church which boasts the impressive 1823 tomb of Lady Catherine Manners and a 9th century Anglo-Saxon cross-head. Also here are the school, a cross bearing an old roadsign, and the lovely rich frontage of the up-market *Peacock Hotel*. This bears a 1652 datestone and was originally a dower house of Haddon Hall: the peacock features on the Manners' coat of arms.

The Post office/shop is on Church Lane, and across from the hotel is a well dated 1841. Down School Lane is Caudwells Mill, a working flour mill dating from 1875 which now incorporates numerous craft workshops. East of the river is the *Grouse & Claret* pub with a camping/caravan site on the riverbank, with the village car park nearby. The former station of the Midland Railway's Derby-Buxton Line was in fact its terminus for some years. Rowsley is the last village on the Wye, which immediately downstream submits to the greater powers of the Derwent.

A well earned pint will do no harm as there remain less than two miles of riverside ambling to walk it off. **Head back along Church Lane but leave at the first chance by a gate on the right. A rough track runs on beneath a railway arch.** Immediately through, look back to see the four-arch viaduct bridging the Derwent. **The track runs on above the river and into an open pasture, cutting a bend of the river before rejoining it for a short enclosed section deep in undergrowth.**

**Shortly after emerging, bear left for a few yards by the river to see it bending away, and our faint way strikes a direct course across the field centres. At the far end it rises more clearly to the bottom corner of the wood. From a stile behind pass along the wallside to approach Calton Lees. Keep left of the buildings to a stile onto the lanehead, and go right through the hamlet.** Several highly attractive buildings are to be seen here. **Swing right on the road which heads away to return to the car park above the garden centre and sawmill.**

*The Peacock, Rowsley*

# 18

# BIRCHEN EDGE

***START*** *Robin Hood* *Grid ref. SK 280721*

***DISTANCE*** *4 miles*

***ORDNANCE SURVEY MAPS***
*1:50,000*
*Landranger 119 - Buxton, Matlock & Dove Dale*
*1:25,000*
*Outdoor Leisure 24 - Peak District, White Peak*

***ACCESS*** *Start from the National Park's Birchen Edge car park at Robin Hood on the B6050, just as it splits from the A619 east of Baslow. A bus stop at the junction is served by Chesterfield-Tideswell and Chesterfield-Bakewell buses. • ACCESS AREA - see page 8.*

The obvious attraction of Birchen Edge is matched by some lovely native woodland, glorious views and a pair of heroic monuments, but there's also a 'sting in the tail' climb in the latter stage of this little gem.

(S) Robin Hood consists of a handful of buildings, most notably the pub, surprisingly known as the *Robin Hood!* There is a small golf course and campsite adjacent. **From the car park head up the back road, briefly, to find a stile set back on the left. Here Open Country is entered and a path doubles back left beneath scattered birch, bracken and heather. Ignoring a first branch clambering clumsily up the bank, advance to the next, less obvious one which rises far more accommodatingly to the heathery beginnings of Birchen Edge.**

Enjoy fine sweeping views over the Derwent Valley, with the cutaway profile of not so distant Curbar Edge prominent. **Go left along the clear path, soon encountering outcrops that lead quickly to Nelson's Monument. This adorns a fine crag top, with the great boulders known as the Three Ships sat on the moorland.**

Nelson's Monument was erected in 1810 to commemorate the great naval hero Admiral Lord Nelson, five years after his death at the great victory of Trafalgar. Its shaft bears the date 1805, and was restored in 1992. The three rocks bears inscribed names of ships in his fleet - *Royal Soverin, Defiant* and *Victory*. Try scrambling up each in turn - the less agile might find Victory forcing them to concede defeat!

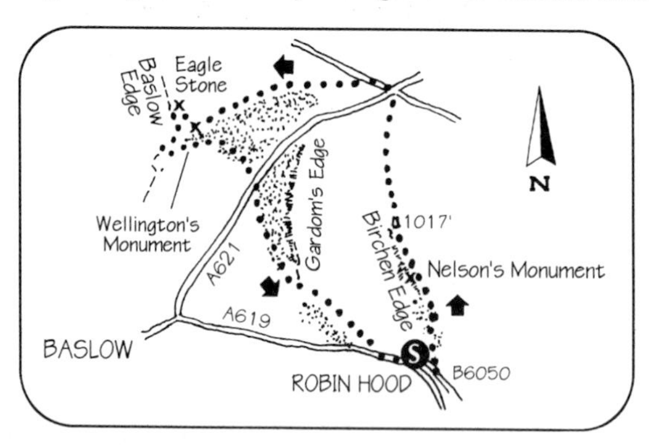


**Forge on to the Ordnance Survey column (S2154) in the heather just beyond.** At a modest 1017ft/310m this marks the summit of the walk. **Continuing, leave the edge path at the last rocks, just beyond, where the heathery path thins and the clearer one drops steeply down to run on to join a broader one. Bear right on this, crossing a heath-like terrain to a crossroads on the A621. Cross straight over and along the Curbar road, but at the first chance go left through a bridle-gate to follow a broad track away.** This is the line of the old Chesterfield-Baslow road, a point confirmed by a tall, inscribed guidepost stood isolated along the wayside.

**The hard track runs on above the trees onto the open moor of Eaglestone Flat. Gently rising, Curbar Edge's profile appears over to the right, and then the massive Eagle Stone ahead. Then just in front, Wellington's Monument appears.** Erected in 1866 (14 years after his death) it commemorates the Duke of Wellington, once the Duke of Rutland's guest on the moor. It stands on a boss of gritstone and marks a splendid viewpoint. With the trees abating it looks out over the side valley of our circuit, across the rolling parkland of Chatsworth to the big house itself, and also back across to Gardom's Edge rising above the trees but below Birchen Edge (illustrated on page 1).

**Here a branch path runs right to the Eagle Stone, a celebrated landmark.** It is said that local young men had to scale this massive boulder before they were eligible to marry: faint hearts and sound minds might suggest that be ample reason for giving it a wide berth! **From it double back left on a broad bridleway to rejoin the old road at a junction. Bear right, back on the old road, running roughly on past old quarries with the beginnings of Baslow Edge just above. As the way drops to a gate off the moor, turn left on a contrastingly narrow path running through bracken above the wallside.**

**Entering an oakwood at the wall-end the path opens out for a super woodland amble, before a return to bracken in a descent through birchwood to the bottom. From a stile descend enclosed to reach a stone arched bridge on Bar Brook.** This old bridge makes a good vantage point for the bizarre environs of the house on the left, which resemble a second-rate Portmeirion!

**A path runs on past some ruins to meet the A621 again. Cross and go left of the cottage opposite, where a stile admits to the kind of country we only just left. A grand path rises through bracken beneath more birchwood, running on by the wood bottom then slanting up through the trees. A splendid holloway climbs up to join us at a gateway in an old wall before our path runs on to a pronounced open knoll alongside one or two minor outcrops.**

With the end in sight this knoll makes a fine vantage point, though one might add further interest by a detour on the path curving back up to the left with an old wall. Passing through a gap at the top the Three Men of Gardom's Edge are found, three sprawling cairns at the start of this gritstone edge. Further along, climbing exploits might be witnessed. The whole of this area was a busy place in Bronze Age times, featuring stone circles, burial cairns and field systems near one of which is a recently restored, rare piece of modest rock art.

**Back at the knoll, resume along the path through the gateway and into a large pasture. To the left is a fine stand of outcrops, while our way runs on through the centre, into a broad gap in the bracken.** Here we pass through the middle of a well defined circular enclosure, again dating from the Bronze Age. Birchen Edge offers a first rate display over to the left. **The path drops down to the bottom left corner to meet the A619. Go left on the welcome footway to finish - a pint or a round of golf?!**

# 19

# STANAGE (NORTH)

***START*** *Hollin Bank, Hathersage*    *Grid ref. SK 237837*

***DISTANCE*** *5¼ miles*

***ORDNANCE SURVEY MAPS***
*1:50,000*
*Landranger 110 - Sheffield & Huddersfield*
*1:25,000*
*Outdoor Leisure 1 - Peak District, Dark Peak*

***ACCESS*** *Start from the National Park's Hollin Bank car park, two miles above the village beneath Stanage Plantation. • ACCESS AREA - see page 8.*

A very easy skyline walk along the magnificent scarp of Stanage Edge, far too good for the modest effort required!

**S** Although Stanage Edge is arrayed directly above the car park (through the trees) this start may raise eyebrows, but be assured it is justified: the approach is a near perfect one. If you insist on an easier start, simply go right along the road to the bend at the plantation at Dennis Knoll.

**Return to the car park entrance and go left along the road to the toilet block. Alongside it a stile sends a stone path down to join a broader one in the trees. Turn down this to emerge into a field. Take the right branch which contours across to a stile above a gate. In the trees just below, left of the farm, is North Lees Hall.** This splendid old hall dates from 1594 and is featured in WALK 9.

**From the stile the path slants down colourful terrain to reach a brook.** On the way down, a stone arch in the field below is all that remains of a Roman Catholic chapel of the 1680s. It was built by the

Eyre family from North Lees Hall, but survived no more than three years before local people took exception and tore it down. **Some flagging takes the path down to a ford on the tiny tree-lined brook.** Across, note the ruins of an old mill upstream, and the preserved milldam up in front. **The path climbs left of the pond and out of the wood. Rise up a couple of fields (via stiles) to a gate preceding a short-lived green way running to the modern dwellings at Green's House.**

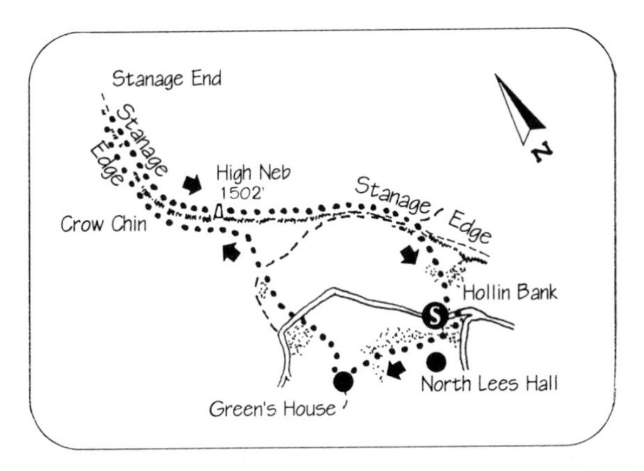


**After the house on the right turn up through a gate, an enclosed old way rising into the trees. At the top the path swings right beneath a bracken bank, passing through a gateway in the adjacent wall then rising with the wall to a stile onto the corner of the moor.** There are grand views over our side valley and down the Derwent Valley, though it is the increasing presence of Stanage just above that takes the eye. **The path rises left across the moorside, running past a plantation to join an open road.**

**Entering Open Country, cross the cattle-grid and cut a corner by taking the path straight over the rough moor to the top end of a small stand of trees. Here we meet the rough road known as the Long Causeway as it climbs to the scarp. Cross straight over to a stile and up a good bracken path towards the edge. Some way short it meets a contouring path. Go left along here, passing a scattering of abandoned millstones before settling down to a superb walk along the base of the scarp.**

Looking across the Derwent Valley we have Kinder Scout overtopping Win Hill (identified by the worn path up its eastern end) with Lose Hill to its right and Mam Tor/Rushup Edge to its left. Shortly Bleaklow also appears ahead, then Ladybower Wood beneath Whinstone Lee Tor. Soon Back Tor comes in straight ahead on Derwent Edge.

*Millstones under Stanage Edge*

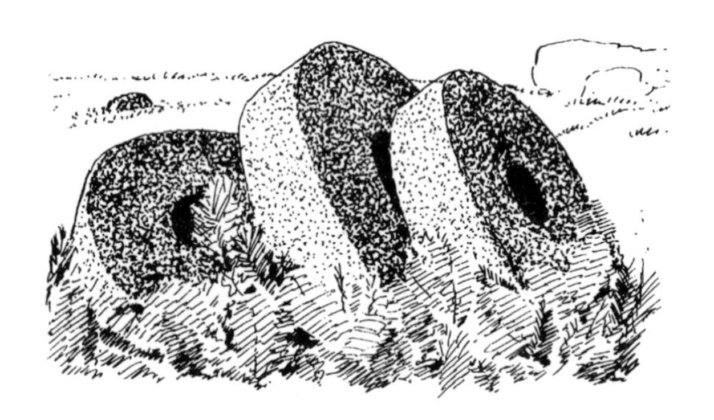

**Beneath the wall of Crow Chin, a branch doubles back up right to reach the crest. One can opt to do likewise, but preferably retain the current path for another half-mile, passing a length of crag-free edge and opening out into heather dominated moor. Approaching the distinctive rocks at Stanage End, fork right and go either side of them to gain the edge.** Ahead now we are looking down on Moscar and the Strines road, with Ladybower Reservoir also appearing.

**All that remains is to double back on the well worn path atop the scarp, set back but able to branch off it at will to explore the drops.** Past a ruined hut on the left all is a rich carpet of heather angling gently away. Spread along the edge is a series of basins hewn from the rocks, some more obvious than others. Each individually numbered, they were created by early 20th century gamekeepers to maintain water supplies for the grouse.

**The super march leads on to the Ordnance Survey column (S2157) at High Neb.** At 1502ft/458m this is the summit of the entire length of Stanage Edge (Peakland's longest), which runs almost four miles from

Stanage End in the north to the Cowper Stone, though the trig. point at the southern end is only inches lower! It is also the finest of the many gritstone edges, with absolutely hundreds of named routes waiting to soak up the climbers taking advantage of its easy access. **Forging on again we soon encounter a short paved section dropping down to a minor nick. In time, shortly after a fence-stile, the thinner path contours along to merge into the old road. Go up this for a moment or two then branch right to resume a contouring path.**

*Stanage Edge from Jacob's Ladder*

**Within a few minutes look out for a flagged path which begins by doubling sharply back down a zigzag to commence a slanting course bound for Stanage Plantation.** This paved trod is known as Jacob's Ladder and is connected with the Long Causeway Roman road that crossed the moor here. The paving itself probably dates from 18th century packhorse use. **The path descends through bracken beneath the crags to enter the woods. Its superb causeyed surface is retained, for the most part, through this delightful scattered woodland, emerging at the bottom directly above the car park.**

20

# CROW STONES

***START*** *Howden Reservoir* *Grid ref. SK 167938*

***DISTANCE*** *6 miles*

***ORDNANCE SURVEY MAPS***
*1:50,000*
*Landranger 110 - Sheffield & Huddersfield*
*1:25,000*
*Outdoor Leisure 1 - Peak District, Dark Peak*

***ACCESS*** *Start from the King's Tree parking area at the Upper Derwent Valley road end. On Summer weekends/BH Mondays the road is closed, but is accessible by a regular bus service from Fairholmes visitor centre. Virtually the whole walk is within the National Trust's Derwent estate, where walkers enjoy open access subject to by-laws.*

A splendid walk in the highest reaches of the Derwent, awash in a sea of moorland broken up by some fine rock outcrops.

**S From the road end pass through the gate and head off along the broad track, crossing the stream out of Linch Clough and maintaining this course for the best part of a mile, the head of Howden Reservoir having faded well before arrival at Slippery Stones bridge.** This 17th century packhorse bridge was saved from the village of Derwent (drowned by Ladybower Reservoir) and re-erected here in 1959: it is illustrated on page 19. This beautiful spot alone is worth the walk. To the vast majority it is their goal, for the young Derwent's bank proves immensely popular with picnickers, sunbathers and paddlers.

**With the trees and crowds left behind, open country beckons. Cross the bridge and take the path upstream, ignoring the bridleway doubling back to the right at a guidepost. Just beyond is a footbridge, the path then bearing right to quickly reach a fork at the foot of**

**Cranberry Clough. Bear left here, remaining on the Landrover track which runs a level course along the main valley floor. Within half a mile take a more inviting, broad green path slanting up to the right.** Gaining height effortlessly it earns fine views into the Derwent's upper reaches.

**A fork is reached by a fence corner.** Here the National Trust operates a woodland regeneration scheme, working to restore some of the native woodland to its rightful place on these steep banks. **Leave the broader modern path climbing away and bear left on a thinner level one, slanting in to cross Broadhead Clough on a small footbridge. Rising away the path reaches a crossroads of seldom trodden old ways. A stile in the fence sends the cross path up from the valley floor.** The cross path was expertly constructed as a shooters' path, as will very shortly be evidenced.

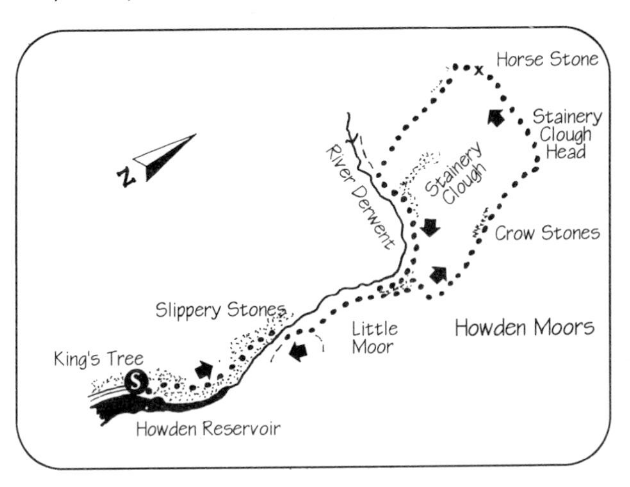


**Ignoring other options double back right up the path's faint but clear upper section, quickly contouring round a nab and running on to the ruins of shooting cabins. The second of these is a base only, with a once clearly valued spring alongside.** Though this may be the one named Lord Edward Howard's Spring, it is often dry, and is usurped by another just beyond, right on the path and gurgling happily even in summer drought. All around, the upper bowl of Broadhead Clough is largely choked by bracken.

**The path fades in the vicinity of the second spring, and though grassy patches twixt bracken are a tempting continuation, it is as easy to climb directly above the spring. The heather slopes are broken by bracken and bilberry, and soon a better defined edge is gained with occasional rock outcrops.** Just a little higher across a broad plateau, and off our route, are the rocks of Outer Edge. **Bear left along our heathery edge to a better cluster of rocks, and a clearer trod now runs on the few minutes to the waiting Crow Stones.**

*At the Crow Stones, looking to Bleaklow*

This is a classic spot in the high Peakland moors. Surrounded by heather, this fine arrangement of sculpted rocks offer unlimited scrambling potential. Two giant ones attract most attention, along with a smaller anvil-type one just below. The view, too, is outstanding, as the upper reaches of the Derwent wind down from the great mass of Bleaklow's eastern end. South-west, Kinder's long skyline overtops a series of intervening ridges. Immediately below is the side valley of Stainery Clough, of which we are about to make a circuit. Note in particular the prominent boulder of the Horse Stone isolated on the moortop opposite: we shall shortly (quicker than it might look) be stood upon it.

**Leave by a well defined trod continuing on heathery slopes beyond the last outcrop to a few scattered rocks.** At this point look back at the Crow Stones to see the anvil-shaped stone in silhouette. **The trod then slants down to Stainery Clough Head, where crossing one stream to a more reedy one, the path fades. Cross beneath the reedy section to a distinct peat patch.** This features a fine example of a decayed tree stump preserved in the peat. **From here a thin path resumes and can be traced around to the beginnings of the widely strewn Horse Stones.**

Looking down to the main valley now, numerous interlocking nabs project, dividing the rolling moorland from the steeper flanks of the river. **The path slants up between the rocks then curves south onto the better defined edge.** The last stone encountered is a curious, perched table top in which of four circular holes, two are complete with outflows. **The Horse Stone is now just ahead, and a trod runs across to it.** In fact it proves to be two stones, or at least a split one. The main rock, however, is a fine boulder offering a simple clamber and several alternative little scrambles. From the top it is interesting to observe the number of trods homing in on this obvious point of convergence.

**Leave by heading south/left, a thin trod leading the couple of minutes to another minor edge, the top of Horse Stone Naze.** This affords the walk's most privileged view into the upper Derwent's highest reaches, backed by a glimpse of the Grinah Stones and the Barrow Stones marking the eastern end of Bleaklow's vast plateau. **Descend left above the various rocks of the well defined edge, the heathery scarp steepening before leaving us on a contrasting plateau.** Up to the left the Crow Stones break the skyline in impressive fashion.

**One could bear left here into the scattered woodland of Stainery Clough, but more easily cross straight over the plateau to descend steep heathery slopes to meet the Landrover track alongside the Derwent.** Here just a mountain stream, it is already carving a deep defile through the moorland. **Turn left, quickly encountering stepping stones at the ford at the base of Stainery Clough, and simply remain on the track to pick up the outward route prior to returning to Slippery Stones and thence the start.**

## LOG OF THE WALKS

| WALK | DATE | NOTES |
|---|---|---|
| 1 | | |
| 2 | | |
| 3 | | |
| 4 | | |
| 5 | | |
| 6 | | |
| 7 | | |
| 8 | | |
| 9 | | |
| 10 | | |
| 11 | | |
| 12 | | |
| 13 | | |
| 14 | | |
| 15 | | |
| 16 | | |
| 17 | | |
| 18 | | |
| 19 | | |
| 20 | | |

# INDEX

***Principal features: walk number refers***

# THE PEAK DISTRICT

**Explore on foot Britain's most popular National Park with a comprehensive set of 5 guidebooks. Each contains 20 walks.**

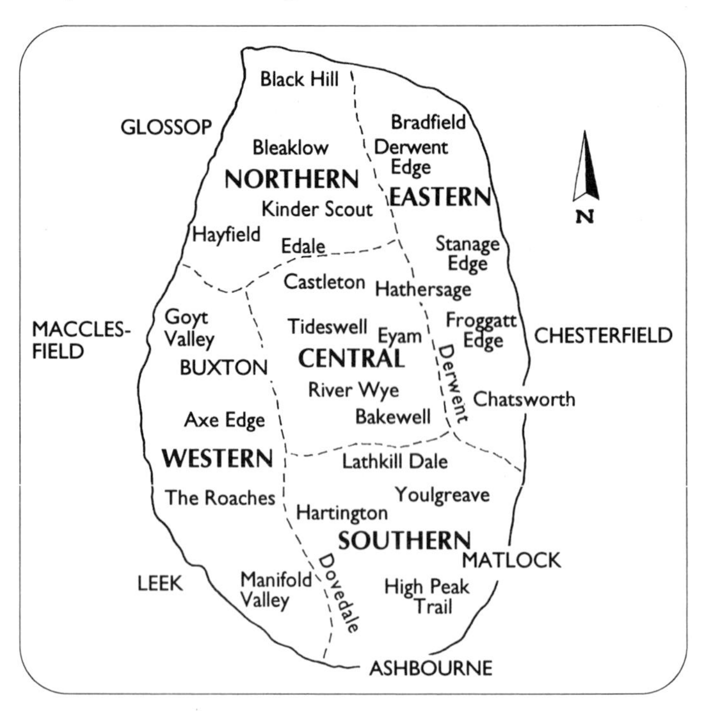


•**NORTHERN PEAK** ISBN 1 870141 48 2
Edale/Kinder Scout/Longdendale/Bleaklow/Hayfield/Mam Tor

•**EASTERN PEAK** ISBN 1 870141 50 4
Derwent Valley/Baslow/Eastern Edges/Chatsworth/Ladybower

•**CENTRAL PEAK** ISBN 1 870141 51 2
Bakewell/Wye Dale/Eyam/Monsal Dale/Tideswell/Miller's Dale

•**SOUTHERN PEAK** ISBN 1 870141 52 0
Dovedale/High Peak Trail/Lathkill Dale/Matlock/Tissington Trail

•**WESTERN PEAK** ISBN 1 870141 54 7
Buxton/The Roaches/Goyt Valley/Manifold Valley/Shutlingsloe